# SHIFTING GEARS AT 50

## A Motorcycling Guide for New & Returning Riders

### By Philip Buonpastore

**With Contributions by Walt Fulton**

**Foreword by David L. Hough**

A Division of BowTie, Inc.
Irvine, CA

**Lead Editor**: Jarelle S. Stein
**Associate Editor**: Jennifer Calvert
**Consulting Editors**: Dave Searle, Scott Rousseau
**Art Director**: Jerome Callens
**Production Supervisor**: Jessica Jaensch
**Assistant Production Manager**: Tracy Vogtman
**Book Project Specialist**: Karen Julian
**Indexer**: Melody Englund

**Vice President, Chief Content Officer**: June Kikuchi
**Vice President, Kennel Club Books**: Andrew DePrisco
**BowTie Press**: Jennifer Calvert, Amy Deputato,
Lindsay Hanks, Karen Julian, Jarelle S. Stein

Library of Congress Cataloging-in-Publication Data

Buonpastore, Philip.
    Shifting gears at 50 : a motorcycle guide for new and returning riders / by Philip Buonpastore ; with contributions by Walt Fulton.
        p. cm.
  Includes index.
 ISBN 978-1-935484-33-2 (pbk.)
 1. Motorcycling. 2. Motorcycles. 3. Motorcyclists. 4. Middle-aged persons--Recreation. I. Title. II. Title: Shifting gears at fifty.
 TL440.5.B86 2012
 629.28'475--dc23
                          2011036628

BowTie Press®
A Division of BowTie, Inc.
3 Burroughs
Irvine, California 92618
www.bowtiepress.com

Printed and bound in China
16 15 14 13 12   1 2 3 4 5 6 7 8 9 10

*For Lora*

# CONTENTS

# Foreword

bumped into Phil a couple years ago at a motorcycle rally, and since then we've had a few "natters" about how motorcycling is changing. Motorcycle journalists are a rare breed, not only traveling by motorcycle but also putting words together that we hope other riders will take to heart. Sometimes we share with each other our writings or our frustrations with getting our thoughts published. Phil consulted with me about his book, because he knew I was a "vintage" rider who had "been there and done that" and was now at an age where I was modifying my riding.

The face of motorcycling is much different today than it was when I started riding back in 1965. Then, lots of youngsters—mostly men—were attracted to motorcycling, and the average age of a motorcyclist in North America was somewhere around twenty-five. Over the years, however, fewer young people have gotten into the sport. Today, the average age of a motorcyclist is about fifty. Among older riders, there are three groups, beginning with those who took up motorcycling in the 1960s and 1970s and just stayed with it and are now are in their sixties and seventies. Then there are those who were happy-go-lucky motorcyclists in their youth but put motorcycling aside while they raised families or developed careers. Today, with more free time and money, they are returning to motorcycling. Finally, there are those of a similar age who didn't ride in their youths but want to learn now. *Shifting Gears at 50* has a great deal of advice for returning and late-entry riders.

I've devoted forty years or so to writing about—and teaching—motorcycling skills. I know that books can help people avoid costly and painful errors and surprises, so I'm especially pleased to see a book focused on returning and late-entry riders. Remember the old saw: "old age and treachery will win out over youth and exuberance." If you're getting into today's motorcycling at an age your doctor would describe as "middle-aged" or "senior," do yourself a clever favor and read Phil's book.

David L. Hough
Author, *Proficient Motorcycling*

# Preface

I bought my first motorcycle when I was forty years old. I had ridden friends' motorcycles and my big brother's dirt bike in my late teens and early twenties but did not have a lot of experience on motorcycles before owning one. At the time I bought my first bike, I had a job in field service that included the use of a company car, and I had a personal vehicle that was generally going unused. Before jumping in and purchasing a motorcycle, I opted to take a basic motorcycle safety class and get a motorcycle endorsement on my driver's license. After passing the course, I sold my personal car, and I bought my first motorcycle—that was the beginning of the life-changing experience of two-wheeled travel.

an impression on me that when I returned home to Atlanta, I wrote an off-the-cuff piece titled "The Two-Wheeled Secret." It was my first attempt at writing a travelogue, and I just tried to capture some of the newfound feelings of unfettered freedom I had experienced when I traveled the open road on a motorcycle. On a subsequent bike trip—another week-long tour well into and throughout Florida—I brought my camera gear along to take photos. This time I intended to write seriously about the travel and possibly get a story published.

When I returned from my vacation, I sat down and wrote the article titled "The Real Florida" (see Travelogue 1, page 109). Then I went to a local bookstore and perused

> ## I bought my first motorcycle [at forty]— that was the beginning of the life-changing experience of two-wheeled travel.

I started to ride as a pastime, gaining miles and experience on the bike, and extending time and riding range whenever I could. I joined several motorcycle clubs, most notably the Southern Cruisers; riding with a group helped me to gain more confidence in my abilities. Riding with the Southern Cruisers, especially on several day-long group rides, also got me comfortable with spending all day on the bike. It was a short jump from there to solo weekend travels and, eventually, from there to longer periods on planned motorcycle vacations.

About a year after I started riding, I took my first week-long, long-distance tour into northern Florida. The experience was overwhelming: the freedom of the ride, the feeling of being part of the environments I rode through, the ability to improvise changes to planned routes to explore interesting rural roads and areas, and the disengagement from the cares of daily life. That tour made such

its magazine racks for periodicals that catered to both the type of travel I was doing (touring) and my type of motorcycle (a cruiser). *Motorcycle Tour and Cruiser* (now *Roadbike*) seemed tailor-made for my style of travel, so I sent my story to the magazine. Three days later, I received a phone call from the editor, Laura Brengleman, telling me she wanted to publish the article! A new career was born, just a few months shy of my forty-first birthday.

That was the start for me. Over the next several years, I toured the southeastern United States on my motorcycle, wrote about the trips, and sold the stories when I could. Eventually, it occurred to me that I had experienced, witnessed, or (in discussions with other riders about their experiences) heard about the majority of problems and pitfalls common to new riders. I felt that I could help new riders deal with issues ranging from how they learned to ride, to what kinds of bikes and gear they might buy, to how to improve their motorcycling skills. I also wanted to encourage new riders and let them know that although learning to ride a motorcycle well would require time and dedication, doing so would definitely be worth the effort. Learning to ride would make possible a whole new world of amazing adventures on the road.

As part of the research for this book, I looked into a number of articles and studies written on the effect of "age-related slowdown" as it corresponds to drivers and motorcycle riders. Although there are certainly studies indicating that age is at least a factor in the safe operation of a vehicle of any type, there are other studies that question these findings and explore the subject

## Being older can even work in your favor if you use what you have acquired over the years—common sense.

I also wanted the book to be geared toward a specific group of would-be riders: the "older but wiser" adults who wanted to learn how to ride for the first time, or those who wanted to return to riding after decades off a motorcycle. I wanted them to know that they weren't necessarily "old dogs" who couldn't learn some "new tricks." So *Shifting Gears at 50* was born.

in greater depth or from a different angle.

One such study, on driver reaction time, is from scholar, researcher, and accident expert Marc Green, who over the past four decades has conducted research on human perception, attention, reaction time, memory, and related areas. Green's reaction-time study is summarized on his website, Human Factors, http://www.visualexpert.com/Resources/reactiontime.html.

Young or old, male or female, Ducati or Buell, it doesn't matter. It's two wheels, delightful scenery, pleasant roads, and great camaraderie!

The Moki Dugway in Utah is a challenging ride, but the reward is a superb view of Monument Valley from the top. Many wonders lie ahead for adventurous riders.

In his reaction-time study, Marc Green states:

Although most basic research finds that older people respond slower than younger ones, the data on older drivers' braking times are not entirely clear. One problem is that different studies have used different definitions of older; that is, sometimes "older" means 55, sometimes it could mean 70. Moreover, some studies find no slowing of reaction time with age. Instead, they conclude that the older driver's greater experience and tendency to drive slower compensate all or in part for the decline in motor skills. Nevertheless, I would place the slowing with age to be about 0.3 seconds for a [driver] 65–70. [Yet] older drivers generally compensate for slower reaction times with reduced speeds.

The point is that age doesn't automatically preclude you from learning to ride a motorcycle. The ability to skillfully and safely operate a motorcycle, like the ability to drive a car, depends on your physical and mental fitness, not the year on your birth certificate. Being older can even work in your favor if you use what you have acquired over the years—common sense. Most likely, as an experienced driver, you have become better able to anticipate traffic problems and dangerous driving situations, and you know how to deal with them or avoid them. You also have too much common sense to create them.

Whether you're a new rider or one who's returning to riding after a long hiatus, take that common sense and apply it to riding a motorcycle to become a knowledgeable, capable, and competent rider who can look forward to years of riding adventures.

# Introduction: The Bug

It's a perfect spring day, with comfortable temperatures and a deep blue, cloudless sky. You're driving your car along a familiar rural highway and come over a rise in the road to see a dozen or more headlights coming your way. As a group of motorcycles rides past, the volume of each bike's engine rises and falls in quick succession, with the Doppler effect changing the pitch of the engine from higher to lower. Sunlight momentarily flashes off the polished chrome as reflection angles change, and it takes your frame of mind from complacency to rapt attention. You find yourself wanting to look at each bike as it passes, but you force your attention back to your own driving. You've seen groups of riders before, and you've always been intrigued by the idea of being part of such a group, but you have no idea how to make that happen. In a few moments, the group disappears from your rearview mirror, and you begin to wonder: Is this something I can do?

For the past twenty years or more, you've worked to advance a career, pay a mortgage and the bills, perhaps raise a family and pay for college tuition, and put money away in a 401(k). Now you're finding yourself with more time and disposable income than you've had in many years. Retirement, or anything like it, is still many years away, and you've never thought of yourself as the couch-potato type. You know that you should take on new interests, but you don't know what direction to go. You've never owned a motorcycle before, or if you did, it was a smaller bike that you had when you were a kid. You may have used it for commuting to high school or an after-school job, but you never really considered it much more than an inexpensive and basic mode of transportation. It's been so long since you've been on a motorcycle that the memories and skills have faded. Still, you wonder. You find yourself looking at motorcycles for sale. You walk past a dealership and make an unplanned detour inside. When a salesperson asks if he or she can help, you say, "No thanks, just looking around."

Whether you know it or not, these are the symptoms of the motorcycling bug, and every rider you saw on the road that day started his or her riding adventures where you are right now. The only difference between those riders and you is that they took the steps to move from thinking how cool riding a motorcycle would be to actually getting on a bike.

Maybe you think it's too far out there to consider riding a motorcycle at this point in your life. Perhaps you think your age is a barrier. Yet a survey done in 2004 by the Motorcycle Industry Council found that 50 percent of new motorcycle riders were over age forty, with 25 percent of them being fifty or older; the percentage

> **The only difference between those riders and you is that they took the steps to move from thinking how cool riding a motorcycle would be to . . . getting on a bike.**

of new riders over forty has increased every year since the survey. Men and women of all ages (women now make up 15 percent to 18 percent of all riders, and those numbers are on the rise, as well) are out there enjoying the sport, so what makes them different from you?

Motorcycle riding does require physical and mental competence, but statistics indicate that these are typically not limiting factors for a healthy "middle-age" adult (sorry, I hate that expression, too). As long as you are in fairly good health, there's no reason why age should be a barrier. One of my favorite old jokes is about a guy who walks up to a pianist and says, "You know, I've always wanted to play the piano, but I'm fifty now." And the pianist replies, "Well, how old would you be if you didn't learn how to play?"

# PART 1

# BECOMING A MOTORCYCLIST

# CHAPTER 1

# LEARNING TO RIDE

» Consider *Shifting Gears at 50* as your road map to becoming a skilled motorcycle rider and your ticket to the fascinating and exhilarating world of motorcycling. This portion of the map will help you navigate around the first obstacles you encounter when learning to ride a motorcycle, including common mistakes that are frequently made by new and returning riders. Among these mistakes can be the method you choose to learn to ride.

To understand the advantages (and the disadvantages) of one method of learning over another, let's start by reviewing a bit about the history of motorcycling and motorcycle licensing in the United States.

# How It Was and How It Is

The popularity of motorcycling increased in the United States in the 1960s and 1970s with the influx of lightweight, stylish, and relatively inexpensive Japanese motorcycles, which usually required less maintenance and could be started with the push of a button (instead of the sometimes-exhausting kickstarter). Sales of these bikes were helped by well-executed advertising campaigns ("You meet the nicest people on a Honda").

Like today, people then were attracted to motorcycling not only as an exciting hobby or sport but also as an economical means of transportation. The advent of the oil crisis in 1973 certainly added to the interest in motorcycles. Unlike today, however, motorcycle licensing requirements in the 1960s and 1970s were minimal, and how you learned to ride was pretty much catch-as-catch-can.

## Ride Now and Learn Later

When I started riding in my home state of Florida in the 1970s, anyone fifteen years old or older could ride a small motorcycle with what was called a restricted operator's license. The restricted license was issued after a person passed a short written test on the rules of the road. The restricted license was the precursor for an operator's license, which could be obtained at the age of sixteen. Even those who kept the restricted license could ride motorcycles of any size after turning sixteen. There were no motorcycle-specific tests.

## Streetmasters Advice from *Walt Fulton*

# Is Motorcycling for You?

Wondering if this sport is for you? Here are some questions to ask yourself and the reasons to ask them:

■ Can you ride a bicycle? This is a simple question, but balance is crucial to successful motorcycling and is a requirement if you want to take a basic course from the Motorcycle Safety Foundation (MSF) or similar organizations. If you haven't ridden a bicycle for a while and need a refresher, spend time on one to refine your balance. Don't forget that bicycling is also excellent exercise.

■ Optional but helpful: Have you driven an automobile with a manual transmission (clutch)? Knowing how to use a clutch is not required—a lot of people who've never learned to drive with one have become successful riders—but it will certainly give you a leg up when it comes to understanding and effectively using the friction zone (when the clutch is only partially engaged, giving you more control over the power to the rear wheel).

■ Can you stay focused? Motorcycling requires your full attention, 100 percent of the time. Riding is not a good time to let your mind wander to your day at the office or that home remodeling project.

■ Do you exercise good judgment? This is as important as good technique. The rider with a

You must be able to ride a bicycle before taking a motorcycle course.

"me first," instant-gratification attitude may not have the responsibility and patience to exercise the necessary restraint. Risk taking on two wheels is not a smart option. Motorcycling is very unforgiving to individuals who like to live on the edge!

This 1976 Honda CR250R belonged to self-taught rider Ed Snow (*see pages 46–47*), who raced with his "lean, mean, fast, screaming, riding machine." He loved the sport but felt his skills suffered for want of a mentor.

I hark back to this piece of history to show how easy it once was, not only in Florida but in most other states, to hop on a motorcycle and ride off into the sunset. There were no organizations offering motorcycle training on proper riding technique nor states requiring a rider to pass a motorcycle skills test to get a license. People assumed that operating a small motorcycle for a year would be sufficient training for riding larger ones—that riders could gain the necessary experience for controlling a bike and dealing with traffic on their own. The idea was that on a small bike, any mishaps would be less severe than on a larger, more powerful bike.

**Learn First and Live Longer**

The need for a greater level of rider training gave rise to the concept of motorcycle safety programs, and in 1973, the Motorcycle Safety Foundation (MSF), a national nonprofit organization, was established and began offering training courses for riders. The idea that this type of training was necessary was reinforced eight years later, when University of Southern California researcher H. H. (Harry) Hurt and his team published a motorcycle-safety study titled *Motorcycle Accident Cause Factors and Identification of Countermeasures.*

This study (now known, ironically enough, as the Hurt Report) investigated roughly 900 motorcycle accidents and analyzed data on 3,600 others in the Los Angeles area from 1975 to 1980. One of most notable accident statistics as it relates to motorcycle-rider training is this: "The motorcycle riders involved in accidents are essentially without training; 92 percent were self-taught or learned from family or friends." A review of the latest federal accident statistics shows that a lack of rider training still contributes to motorcycle accidents.

Today, all fifty states require a motorcycle license or a motorcycle endorsement on an existing driver's license to legally operate a bike. Insurance companies will not insure a motorcycle or a rider without one, so before a rider gives any consideration to the purchase of a motorcycle, he or she must obtain a motorcycle license or endorsement.

# Two Routes to Licensing

There are two routes to obtaining a motorcycle license or endorsement. The first one is the do-it-yourself method, and the second one is a professionally taught option, which takes a safer and more strategic approach to learning to ride. This second option is the one more likely to keep you on a motorcycle for a long time.

I wouldn't have lent my BMW R1150RT—which I bought after gaining some years of riding experience—to the novice me to practice on!

### Route 1: The Rocky Road

Because most states offer a temporary motorcycle learner's permit to any licensed motorist, you can go to your local state Department of Motor Vehicles (DMV) or Motor Vehicle Commission (MVC) office to get a permit (you may have to take a written test), borrow or buy a motorcycle, and then start practicing. You can either teach yourself to ride or enlist the help of

## Streetmasters Advice from *Walt Fulton*

# Mentoring

At first blush it may appear that the job of a mentor is an easy one, that any experienced rider should be able to do it. Yet experience alone does not make for a good teacher.

In motorcycling, a mentor should be not only an expert motorcyclist but also someone who can offer meaningful counsel, suggestions, direction, and sources of information with as little personal bias as possible. It's imperative that this person be able to listen objectively to the preferences of the learner and be able to clearly evaluate his or her needs.

Too often, when someone is teaching a spouse or other family member, giving truly objective counsel is difficult. Keep in mind, too, that the very process of mentoring can be more difficult when you're working with a family member—one or both of the parties are more likely to become impatient, irritated, or upset.

If you decide to seek someone to help instruct you, make sure that person is qualified for the job. Ask potential mentors how many miles they ride in a year on average, what types of bikes they have owned, and what types of riding they have done. High mileage and experience with a variety of bikes and types of riding are good qualifications for a mentor. Real veterans are less likely to be biased against the type of bike or riding you might like to have or do.

All good mentors have one other very important qualification: they use positive reinforcement, rather than criticism, to help you learn.

an experienced rider. When you think you've mastered the basic motorcycle skills, you return to the DMV/MVC and take the written test (if you didn't take it to get the permit) and the riding-skills test to get a motorcycle license or endorsement.

Realistically, if you're a first-time rider or have been off a motorcycle for a long time, this route can prove to be a pricey, dicey, and inefficient proposition. To begin with, few, if any, experienced riders will want to lend their pride and joys to an inexperienced or returning rider. Even if you find someone who is willing to do so, the bike will probably be unsuitable for you as a learner (too tall, too heavy, too powerful).

If you cannot get a loaner, you may have to purchase your own bike—probably before you have gained any real riding experience, before you have acquired enough experience to know what kind of bike to buy, or even before you know if you are going to enjoy riding long term. There is also the danger of learning improper riding techniques, either from attempting to teach yourself or from the coaching of a well-meaning friend or family member.

There is one other option now available for taking the riding-skills test at the DMV/MVC. If you have your permit, you can rent a small motorcycle (250cc or smaller) or a small scooter from one of the businesses that rent them out for the sole purpose of helping you pass the test. At the time you're scheduled to take the riding test, someone from the rental business will meet you at the DMV/MVC with a motorcycle or scooter.

For an extra charge, some of these rental companies offer to give you a short period of instruction on riding the bike or scooter. If you go this route, you will get *only* enough instruction to pass the test on a small bike or scooter. Such an arrangement may get you a motorcycle license, but that's all it will do. It will not teach you how to ride safely or give you crucial information on important techniques such as strategic braking and countersteering. (See Licensing Requirements and Courses for details on what various courses offer, pages 24–26.)

Terry Vinyard
and his Suzuki Intruder

## »» A Rider's Tale
# Terry's Story: Clutches and Perseverance

I first got the bug to ride after my divorce in 2005, at age thirty-five. I'd never really thought about motorcycling before, but suddenly I found myself thinking about motorcycles and imagining myself on one. I had some friends and coworkers who rode, and I started asking them a lot of questions. The best piece of advice that I received was to take a riding class. It just so happened that there was a Harley-Davidson dealership just up the road from my apartment that offered the Rider's Edge beginning class.

My main concern before starting the class was that I'd never driven a car with manual transmission and so didn't know how to use a clutch. People assured me that it wouldn't make much difference. Wrong! The first day on the bike, I fell three times because I couldn't get used to the clutch. But I told myself that if I really wanted to do this, this was the time and the place. I ended up passing the class, getting 100 percent on my written test, and passing my riding test—in the pouring rain, no less.

About six months later, I bought a 2003 Suzuki Intruder, a great starter bike, and have never looked back. I enjoy riding to and from work, making an occasional excursion to the mountains, and exploring unknown roads. I've even learned to do my own oil changes and general maintenance. Motorcycling has been all I imagined and more.

Students in this Motorcycle Safety Foundation Basic RiderCourse ride small loaner motorcycles and wear loaner full-face helmets. Most, if not all, basic riding courses offer use of equipment to the novice rider, a distinct advantage.

## Route 2: The Strategic Road

Fortunately for you, there's a better route than those just described: a basic riding course taught by certified instructors. These courses can be found all over the country. In the past four decades, the MSF, which conducts rider training in forty-eight states, has successfully taught more than 3 million people how to ride. Oregon and Idaho feature their own state-sponsored rider training programs: Team Oregon and Idaho STAR (Skills Training Advantage for Riders).

I took the MSF Basic RiderCourse when I began riding again in 1996; it was a two-and-a-half-day, fifteen-hour course that cost $150 and offered at a Honda corporate location in Alpharetta, Georgia. As of the writing of this book, the cost for the MSF course, depending on where you take it, ranges from free in Illinois and Pennsylvania to $350 in New York. For your money, you get:

■ A motorcycle to ride—theirs, not yours. This loaner motorcycle is typically a 250cc, which is big enough for you to get started on. You also get the use of a helmet approved by the Department of Transportation (DOT).

■ Classroom training with instruction on techniques to maximize personal safety and situational awareness on the road.

■ Actual experience on a riding course, where you will become familiar with (or reintroduced to) motorcycle controls and their operation and have an opportunity to learn basic maneuvers, such as smooth engagement of the clutch, proper techniques for turning and handling the bike, and smooth stopping.

For the riding portion of the class, you will be given a list of protective clothing you need to wear; items will likely include a sturdy jacket and pants, over-the-ankle leather boots with oil-resistant high-traction tread, leather gloves that cover the entire hand, and protective eyewear—all items you will need when you begin riding anyway. *Note:* you will want to purchase motorcycling-specific riding gloves once you have passed the class, but until then, a pair of leather full-coverage gloves should work.

Going this route is well worth the reasonable cost of a class. You not only learn about the proper operation of a motorcycle but also receive excellent information on riding techniques, motorcycle safety, operating the bike in traffic, and other motorcycling subjects that you would not get as a self-taught rider (or one given minimal instruction by a bike rental company). For those who have previous experience on a motorcycle but rode before licensing was required, this is still a great opportunity and an inexpensive way to dust off and update skills prior to taking to the road again.

Cathy Siglow took the strategic road to relearn how to ride in her fifties.

## >>> A Rider's Tale
# Cathy's Story (Part 1): The Wrong Teacher

When Bob and I got married, he was buying small motorcycles, fixing them up, and reselling them. We had ridden together through Europe with me on the back, and when I decided that I wanted to ride my own bike, Bob figured he could teach me. The bikes I used usually didn't work smoothly, but he always felt the problem was with me, not the bike. This mentoring process ended up being a very traumatic and emotional experience for both of us, but we somehow managed to get through it. I got the motorcycle endorsement on my license and started riding a 125, then a 250, then a 350, and then, just before Bob and I divorced, a Honda CB500.

I was riding the 500 when I met my second husband, Jess. He had mostly done off-road riding, but he bought a street bike just to ride with me. I had been riding for eight years and I had accumulated about 10,000 miles by the time our first son was born. I put away my motorcycle then, knowing I had a responsibility to raise my child to adulthood and self-sufficiency and could no longer take unnecessary risks.

Fast-forward twenty-three years: In fall 2003, our oldest son's fiancée, Jen, informed me that she wanted to learn to ride a motorcycle and asked me to take the MSF class with her. As our youngest son was now twenty-two years old and a Green Beret, obviously able to take care of himself, I said yes. Taking a class from trained instructors sounded like a good idea. From my past experience (remember Bob?), I knew that learning a technical skill from a family member was not a good idea.

The class proved to be interesting and fun, but I discovered I had to unlearn several very bad habits. Jen, three other women, and I were not able to pass the class on the first go-round, which made me realize just how bad a rider I had been in my younger days.

The school set up a weekend for the five of us to work with a female instructor on the areas in which we were deficient. Our instructor was patient, but she still expected us to reach an acceptable level of skill. We spent two days on the bike range improving our skills and were then able to pass the course and get our licenses. [See chapter 5 for the second part of Cathy's story.]

A Motorcycle Safety Foundation instructor puts students through cornering drills. Cornering is a critical skill, taught in all beginner courses and improved on in advanced courses and specialty schools, such as Streetmasters Motorcycle Workshops, where Walt Fulton is lead instructor.

# Licensing Requirements and Courses

Check your state's motor vehicles website to learn what's required for licensing and motorcycle operation in your state. Some states require residents to take a basic riding course before they can obtain a motorcycle license. A basic riding course ends with a written knowledge test and a riding-skills test. If you can pass those two tests, you will receive a certificate that you present to your local DMV/MVC, which then waives the requirement to take the riding-skills test and, in the majority of cases, the written test. (Check with your state's DMV/MVC to find out whether you still need to take a written test at one of its offices.) Often, insurance companies will lower motorcycle insurance premiums for individuals who have completed a riding course.

### Basic Courses

Many places offer basic rider training, including college campuses and the corporate locations of motorcycle manufacturers as well as dealerships and privately owned sites. Programs may be conducted by the MSF, by Harley-Davidson or another manufacturer, or by independent state-sponsored rider organizations, such as Team Oregon and Idaho STAR. Most rider-training organizations offer more than one level of basic rider training. An Internet search will find places sponsoring state-approved classes.

Harley-Davidson's basic riding course, called the Rider's Edge, is also taught by instructors

### Returning Rider Courses

In 2011, the MSF added new courses, among them one specifically for returning riders. To take the course, you must have a permit and basic riding skills. The course covers elements of both the first- and second-level basic courses. As a returning rider, you may find that the faster pace of this type of course is more to your liking.

Perhaps you rode a larger displacement motorcycle back in the day, so the idea of taking a class using a 250cc or smaller motorcycle on a closed riding course is a bit of a strain on your ego. After all, some of the instructors teaching the class were probably in diapers when you first rode. If you were a rider after motorcycle licensing requirements began, you may even still have an M endorsement on your driver's license, kept through the years "just in case." So, do you really need to take this class? The answer is a resounding "Yes!" Knowledge about riding and riding techniques has come a very long way in a generation or two, as have motorcycle styles, power, handling, and amenities. It makes good sense to update your skills with the best information and training available by taking a basic riding course.

This is an opportunity to get used to riding again in a closed environment, which will help ensure that you can comfortably ease back into riding and relearn riding techniques. Just as important, the course offers you the chance to unlearn some bad techniques

certified by MSF but covers some Harley-Davidson-specific content. The Rider's Edge course currently uses larger displacement motorcycles in its training classes (the Buell Blast 500cc single). Whether this course is for you depends on your preferences, goals, and comfort zone. These classes are generally a bit more expensive than other riding courses, and in some cases require that you bring a DOT-approved helmet. Graduates of this course also receive a licensing endorsement certificate upon completion.

Basic courses, no matter who teaches them, use a common curriculum that exposes new and returning riders to fundamental riding information, including safety, proper riding technique, and a specific set of criteria and goals necessary for the competent operation of a bike. Besides making the licensing procedure a smooth, educational, and efficient process, the basic riding class is just plain fun.

## Consider This

To legally ride a motorcycle, you will be required to take a motorcycle-specific written test and a riding-skills test of some type. Whether you take the tests through an established training program or by going directly to the DMV/MVC, you must get a license before you can move forward. Why not choose the most efficient way by taking a state-approved basic riding class?

The Suzuki QuadSport Z250 shown here is a popular ATV. Before riding out on a quad, take an ATV-specific course.

you may have picked up as a self-taught rider. You're older and wiser now—don't let ego get in the way of a smart decision.

## Advanced and Other Courses

Many rider-training organizations provide advanced courses for riders of every level, as well as training courses in the safe operation of three-wheeled motorcycles, a popular option for older riders. The MSF sponsors classes that include a half-day introductory scooter course and classes for dirt-bike riders as well as for all-terrain vehicles (ATVs). MSF's website, www.msf-usa.org, as well as the websites for other state-specific training organizations such as Team Oregon (http://teamoregon.orst.edu/) and Idaho STAR (www.idahostar.org), contains information on these courses and course curricula.

## A Win-Win Situation

Now you've obtained a motorcycling license, and it is a proud day—I remember! Still, there is more to learn and several decisions to make before you will be ready to ride off into that sunset. The following chapters will help guide you through the next steps to becoming a skilled rider.

Even if you take a course and decide that riding is not for you, you will have learned a good deal about motorcycling, which will increase your awareness of riders when you are driving and give you insight into problems they must contend with on the road. The course will also offer you information on techniques and road safety that will sharpen your driving skills. Whether you choose to continue riding, taking the course is a win-win situation.

## Streetmasters Advice from *Walt Fulton*

# Turning and Countersteering

It is intuitive to rotate a steering wheel to the left and expect the vehicle to turn to the left. Ditto for a right turn. As long as you don't overthink the instructions for turning a motorcycle, doing so is also simple: press forward on the left handlebar to go left and press forward on the right handlebar to go right. The problem begins when you realize that as you press forward on the left handlebar the front wheel turns to the right and on the right handlebar, to the left. Now what you're doing seems counterintuitive. So what's happening? Nothing that geometry and physics can't explain.

But going that route is more complex than necessary for our purposes, so let us try to make it simpler and easier to visualize. This will involve balancing a kitchen broom in your palm. Put the top of the handle on your palm and the business end of the broom up. You will have to move your hand left, right, forward, and back to keep the broom's center of gravity positioned directly over the point on your palm where the handle rests. Once you get the feel of balancing the broom, you should be able to hold it nearly still. At this point, move your hand to the left. Which way does the broom fall? How about when

you move your hand to the right? In the opposite direction of your movement each time, correct?

The association between a broom and a motorcycle may not be obvious at first, but consider it this way: Visualize the broom handle in your hand as the tires' contact patch and your palm as the pavement. It's not quite the same dynamic, but as with a motorcycle, you are "steering" the front wheel out from under the bike's center of gravity, causing it to lean. It's important to understand that motorcycles only turn by leaning, so as you press forward on the left handlebar, the front wheel turns to the right and the bike must lean to the left; you *countersteer* in the direction you want to go.

Let's emphasize this point again: a motorcycle will turn only by leaning; this is why a motorcycle's tire profiles are rounded and not flat like a car's. Regardless of make, model, or country of origin, all motorcycles behave in a similar manner. So, why doesn't your motorcycle continue to fall to the side, finally hitting the ground, when you initiate a lean?

This is the reason: as you relax your forward push on the handlebar, the front wheel will automatically try to center itself; as it does, your arc is stabilized,

the motorcycle doesn't lean any farther or straighten up, and you and it will continue through the corner at your chosen lean angle. Press more on the inside bar, and the motorcycle leans over more. Press on the outside bar, and the bike tends to right itself.

There are some misconceptions about motorcycle steering. Many riders who follow the so-called expert advice of friends and even of some credentialed (but somewhat misinformed) instructors continue to believe that all they do is shift their weight from one side of the motorcycle to the other to initiate a lean and using the handlebar isn't necessary.

In reality, just as with a bicycle that is ridden with "no hands," a motorcycle will turn using weight shifts, but the turn is far from precise and the motorcycle's slow response to this technique can cause real problems for the rider, who must change directions quickly. The classic accident scenario is a rider surprised by a driver turning across the rider's path. At such times, relying on weight shift to alter course will take more time than circumstances allow. You must understand countersteering so that you employ it routinely and can apply it without delay.

# CHAPTER 2

# BUYING YOUR MOTORCYCLE

» You've completed a basic riding course and gotten a license or an endorsement on your driver's license to legally operate a motorcycle on the street. Now it's time to do a little homework to begin the process of choosing the motorcycle that is right for you.

Choosing a motorcycle is a very personal process. Finding the bike that is right for you is about balancing what is, in your mind's eye, the perfect machine—the one that has exactly the right lines and image—with more down-to-earth considerations of size, ergonomics, performance, and cost. One thing is for sure: pick the right bike and it will make you smile every time you look at it, and you will

## Research Sources

There are many research sources out there with great information on motorcycles and everything to do with motorcycles. Four of them are magazines, books, websites, and dealerships and motorcycle shows. Don't forget one other more important source: your fellow riders (especially those with some years of experience), including your riding instructor.

### Magazines

On the periodical racks in bookstores and elsewhere, you'll find magazines that publish serious, solid, and enjoyable information about riding and traveling on a motorcycle. They include, among many other subjects, reviews on different kinds of bikes, touring and travel articles, reviews of gear for daily use and for travel, and advice on improving riding techniques.

The April 2011 issue of *Motorcycle Consumer News* (like all of the magazine's issues) is packed with good information on bikes, gear, skills, and many other motorcycling subjects. As its website says, *MCN* "is wholly supported by our readers, who expect us to be unswayed by industry influences on reporting."

## ⟫ A Rider's Tale
# Diana's Story: A Perfect Fit

When I was nine, a family friend ("Uncle Bob") who had a motorcycle let me sit on the passenger seat while he rode around the block. Uncle Bob enjoyed hearing me giggle when he increased the throttle a little bit more, and he loved hearing the "wheeeeeeeeeeee" as he leaned the bike into a turn. I didn't know what kind of motorcycle he had; all I knew was that, although the bike was huge and intimidating, it enveloped me and gave birth to my love for motorcycles.

Yet when I was older, I didn't pursue riding a motorcycle; in fact, I didn't give riding another serious until my early forties. One day, I mentioned to a coworker that I was thinking about purchasing a scooter in order to indulge my sense of adventure for beautiful Northern California. She emphatically dissuaded me from a scooter and directed me to a motorcycle because, as she said, "the only part of Northern California a scooter could take you adventuring would be San Francisco."

I was certain I couldn't actually learn how to handle a full-fledged motorcycle until she convinced me that if she could ride one at 5'3" and 115 pounds, nothing should stop me from the challenge. As we surfed the Internet for various bikes, my friend strongly recommended that I get a Kawasaki Vulcan 500 as a starter bike. The bikes used in the motorcycle training course I was taking were 125cc, and she said I would soon grow out of one that size. I sat on the Vulcan 500 and realized that it was very female friendly; the handlebars were the perfect distance to allow a slight bend in the elbow for flexibility, the handlebar height was parallel

As of 2011, probably a dozen well-known periodicals target some segment of the motorcycling public. Some of the periodicals that offer no-nonsense information on many different kinds of motorcycles include *Cycle World*, *Motorcycle Consumer News*, *Motorcycle Cruiser*, and *Rider* magazine. They rank among the better motorcycling magazines thanks to the experienced writers and staff and the information they impart about all aspects of motorcycling.

## Books

Although few motorcycling books have been written especially for new and returning riders in the forty, fifty, and older age group—hey, that's what makes the one in your hands unique!—you can find hundreds on motorcycling, exploring the many facets of the sport. For useful information on choosing and buying a bike, as well as additional gear, there is,

Diana Fierke on her Suzuki
V-Strom 650, which she moved up to in 2011.

to my chest for that feeling of control and help in reducing fatigue, and the seat height allowed me to plant both feet firmly on the ground with a considerable bend in the knee for a sense of security to maintain stability at a stop. The upright position was comfortable on my back—it felt like a living-room lounge chair. As a beginner, I found the Vulcan 500 a perfect fit.

among other helpful works, Bill Stermer's *Streetbikes: Everything You Need to Know* (Motorbooks, 2006).

If you want to further hone your skills after reading *Shifting Gears at 50*, get David Hough's *Proficient Motorcycling* (BowTie Press, 2nd ed., 2008). As the subtitle says, it is the "Ultimate Guide to Riding Well." You can also learn much about what to do and what not to do by reading about other riders' experiences and find out how it feels to be out on the road on a long-distance adventure by reading travel books. You may come to realize that there is no reason you can't be just as adventurous as the author-riders.

## Internet

This source of information is continually expanding. Blogs and websites relating to motorcycling and motorcycle travel are easy to find with a simple Internet search. When you sign up with a riders' discussion group online, you can ask questions of experienced riders. You can ask about good first bikes and get opinions on a specific bike you're thinking about buying. You can find information on gear, events, and great roads, and you can read about other riders' adventures. A world of information, photos, and blogs are only an Internet search away. A few websites you might begin with are webBike World.com and Motorcycle-usa.com; suggested motorcycling-magazine websites to check out include MCNews.com, Ridermagazine.com, and Motorcyclecruiser.com.

*A word of caution*: If you are unfamiliar with an Internet source or unsure of its authenticity, be wary of the information offered. Check several websites in order to obtain as wide a range of opinions as possible, and try to find the most unbiased information out there about any motorcycle or motorcycle product.

## Dealerships and Motorcycle Shows

Of course, somebody's trying to sell you something, but that doesn't mean you have to buy until you know what you want. At a dealership, you have an opportunity that you have few other places—to

The Versys 650cc has been classified as a standard bike, a sportbike, an adventure-tourer. Kawasaki calls it "a jack-of-all trades with user-friendly versatility."

look at and sit on bikes of different types, shapes, and sizes. You can do that at a motorcycle show, too. Depending on the show, you can look over the latest bikes and try them on for fit. The shows range in size from the large annual Progressive International Motorcycle Shows, which visit twelve metropolitan areas annually, to small local shows.

## Types of Bikes

So what kind of motorcycle should you buy? I don't mean which manufacturer, but which category. There are six main categories and many variations within each (hybrids). Then there are the three-wheeled motorcycles, which have been around for years but have recently gained in popularity, especially among older riders.

### Standard Bikes

Standards are the basic platform for motorcycle ergonomic layouts, with relatively comfortable seats, an upright riding position, handlebars that do not require the rider to lean far forward, footpegs in line with the rider's seat, and engines tuned for easy driveability.

Standard motorcycles usually have very little in the way of amenities as stock equipment (for instance, a standard may have either no windshield or a very small one and have few locations for storage). Larger displacement bikes of this type range from powerful to very powerful, generally use twin- or four-cylinder engines, and have a more straight-up seating posture and good handling and cornering capabilities. This style of motorcycle is manufactured as a street bike.

# Nakeds: Defined

Many people use *naked bike* as a synonym for *standard bike*. Others consider nakeds a sub-category of standards. This *naked standard* is said to be derived from the sportbike. Gone are the sportbike's full-coverage aerodynamic bodywork, low handlebars, and highly tuned engine; what remains are its refined chassis geometry and top-quality suspension and brakes in a relatively lightweight upright package with a slightly detuned motor. A naked has greater agility and handling and braking quality than a typical standard. Defined this way, all nakeds are standards but not all standards are nakeds.

## Cruisers

Cruisers mimic the 1950s motorcycle look: a round headlight (or headlights), pulled-back handlebars, a V-twin engine or similar, and chromed pipes, and a straight-up or feet-forward (slightly or very) riding position. Most bikes of this type also incorporate a larger seat with a lower seat height, from as low as 25 inches off the ground, offering riders of almost any stature solid footing. Cruisers' engines usually have lower horsepower but higher torque for increased pull at low RPMs [revolutions per minute] than do standards and sportbikes—a feature that generally allows a more sedate riding experience for the rider.

## Sportbikes

These are racing-style motorcycles with the necessary equipment added to allow them to comply with state and federal laws for street use. Most sportbikes are equipped with extremely powerful multicylinder engines in the 600cc to 1000cc range, which often produce 150 horsepower or more. Sportbikes are designed for extreme acceleration and cornering.

Although they can outperform any other type of bike, sportbikes have a very leaned-forward racing-style riding position that puts increased pressure on the hands, wrists, neck, and lower back. Add to this a higher footpeg location, a smaller seat, and extra-firm suspension, and you have a motorcycle that doesn't usually play well with the over-forty set. The power available with these bikes is also better left to riders with more experience. There's

A Honda Shadow RS cruiser, with a 745cc engine, offers good power, but not too much power, for the beginner.

Great for canyon riding and the track, the agile Suzuki GSX-R750, like most bigger sportbikes, is too powerful and not recommended for the new rider.

nothing wrong with making a wise choice based on your present level of riding experience and what is a more comfortable fit for you.

If you are set on a sportbike, there are a few in the 250cc range, such as Honda's CBR250R (see pages 40–41). These bikes are lighter and less powerful, making them better choices for a new or returning rider.

In general, sportbikes are not intended for long-distance travel. The sport-touring motorcycle, however, brings sportbike performance to bikes with storage capabilities for such travel. Although the sport-touring bike does not have as severe a riding position, it is still designed with a high level of performance, and its greater weight makes it a challenge for some riders. It is not a good first-bike choice. I have owned a sport-touring motorcycle and appreciated its exceptional performance and long-distance traveling capabilities, but I did not buy it until I had been riding for more than five years.

## Touring Motorcycles

Usually the largest and heaviest motorcycles, touring bikes are designed to cover long distances, and

A rider hits the dirt on his BMW R1200GS adventure bike. Not a beginner's bike, but one that may be worth working up to.

they typically have plenty of storage room and user-friendly travel features and amenities. These often include trip-computer functions, such as average and instantaneous gas mileage and distance to empty, and may include GPS navigation and sound systems. Provided that your experience as a rider grows over time, a full-size touring bike may be in your future, but I advise against one, which is usually well in excess of 800 pounds unloaded, as a first bike.

## Adventure Motorcycles

An adventure motorcycle is a do-everything motorcycle, a rugged machine engineered to travel on streets and on highways as well as on unpaved and backcountry terrain. The larger versions can be equipped with a generous amount of storage capacity in large hard or rigid saddlebags and are

With the K1600GT, *Motorcycling News* says, "BMW has created a supersports touring bike that adds . . . sex appeal." Not for the novice rider.

The dual-sport Husqvarna TE449 is designed for on-road and off-road riding.

ideal if you intend to travel across Australia's outback or through Africa. Of course, they would also work fine for a tour across America or Europe. The capabilities of these very versatile motorcycles, however, are probably a bit outside what a first-time or returning rider would require. Still, if you're planning to ride across Africa . . .

## Dual-Sport Bikes

As the name implies, the dual-sport bike is a motorcycle designed for both on- and off-road use. This type of motorcycle is generally not ideal for street riding, but because it is designed with a headlight and a taillight, you can legally ride it on the road and use it off-road, as well, exploring dirt roads and trails that otherwise might only be accessible by vehicles with four-wheel drive. The dual-sport bike is more practical than a pure dirt bike, which must be

transported to a designated off-road riding area by truck or by trailer.

Even if you don't have any interest in riding off-road, you may want to consider taking one of the dirt-bike-riding classes now offered by many organizations. Dirt riding can be a good way to practice riding techniques you use in street riding. (See Riding Off Road, page 74, for further discussion.)

## Consider This

Some beginning riders may want to think about buying a lightweight dual-sport bike for its easy handling and the fact that it allows you to learn and practice advanced skills in an area without traffic (off-road).

Operator and passenger enjoy the comfort and greater stability of this three-wheeled motorcycle, the Can-Am Spyder RT-S. Three-wheeled motorcycles are especially favored by older riders who are concerned about supporting the weight of a two-wheeled bike, balancing the bike, and carrying a passenger on it.

## Three-Wheeled Motorcycles

In a category of their own are the three-wheeled motorcycles (also called motorized tricycles or trikes), which are typically conversions from large touring motorcycles (such as Honda Gold Wings, H-D Electra Glides, and Victory Visions). This type of trike is usually configured with one wheel in the front and two in the rear. In his *Wall Street Journal* article "The Easy Rider: Baby Boom Bikers Defect to the Trike" (November 5, 2007), Jonathan Welsh writes:

> After decades of being dismissed as fringe vehicles, trikes are gaining favor with baby boomers confronting the realities of old age, from knee injuries and arthritis to a diminished sense of balance. Motorcycles may forever symbolize youthful rebellion, but trikes . . . are a lot easier to maneuver in stop-and-go traffic.

If you have a real desire to ride a motorcycle but have concerns about being able to (among other requirements) support a bike's weight, balance the bike while riding and stopping, and carry a passenger, consider the trike. Although trikes are usually more expensive than standard motorcycles, they have many advantages in addition to the stability of three wheels: they are larger and wider, with the rear half resembling an automobile more than a bike; they usually have large trunks and increased storage space; and they have a rear-light configuration more closely related to that of a car. Because of that last feature, a three-wheeler is likely to be more visible in traffic (making riding them that much safer). The latest in motorized three-wheelers is the Can-Am Spyder, which has two wheels in the front and a single wheel behind. Purpose built (rather than a conversion), it offers more stability and enhanced control.

Advanced rider classes are available for three-wheeled motorcycle riders. As always, it's a good idea to take a class and get some specific instruction targeted to the idiosyncrasies of piloting a three-wheeler. There's more to it than a trike not needing a kickstand. The technique for cornering, for one, is very different on three wheels than on two.

# Recommended First Bikes

Yes, there are many types of motorcycles to choose from, but some are better choices for a first motorcycle than others are. You may be thinking that if you're going to spend money on a bike, you should get as much performance as you can. That's an understandable approach, but remember that at this stage you're still learning and refining basic motorcycle skills. You want a bike that you can handle and operate effectively and comfortably; it should be a good fit for your height, build, and skill level. Your first motorcycle should be one you can grow on (that is, perfect your basic skills on), but keep in mind that first bikes are not meant to be last bikes. You dream bike can wait a little longer until you've built up the skills to ride it.

For a first bike, I recommend a cruiser. Although cruisers of 1200cc and above can be on the heavy side, new and returning riders should be able to easily handle the smaller (and lighter) models. For the novice or returning rider, Walt Fulton, of Streetmasters Motorcycle Workshops (see Walt's advice boxes throughout the book), recommends standards of 800cc or less, which are lighter and have greater handling capabilities than other types of bikes.

## Cruiser Advantages

A cruiser engine generally has lower horsepower and higher torque than most other types of motorcycles do. A cruiser's power range and torque characteristics will typically have a less abrupt throttle response than do those of performance bikes, which make acceleration smoother and easier to modulate.

A cruiser's engine is typically designed to develop higher torque at a lower engine rpm than engines of sportier bikes. This means the bike's engine will generally be more forgiving when a rider shifts gears outside of the peak power range; this also means the bike will be easier to get moving from a stop, which helps minimize engine

stalling while the rider gets used to the bike. All are positives for new and returning riders.

In addition, most modern-day cruisers in the 650cc to 1300cc displacement range typically have seat heights of 25 to 30 inches, which means you can place both feet firmly on the ground (with knees unlocked) when the bike is stopped, allowing the strongest muscles in the leg to support the bike. You'll find it a much more comfortable feeling than being on your toes. This configuration also contributes to a lower center of gravity that aids in slow-speed stability. As a result, these motorcycles are typically easier to manage and more comfortable for a first-time or returning rider. This type of cruiser motorcycle is usually referred to as a *middleweight* cruiser.

Some caution should be exercised here, as some of the middleweight cruiser models can be fairly large and heavy bikes. As a new or returning rider, you probably should consider cruisers with a weight of less than 700 pounds. Many models in this size range have an engine size that can comfortably handle most riding situations and weigh in the 500 to 600 pound range, making them easier to handle.

Many models of this variety are produced with a factory-added windshield and lockable saddlebags, and often with floorboards rather than footpegs. These are generally called touring cruisers. Getting

This Honda Shadow RS, a middleweight cruiser, has a seat height of 29.3 inches and a wet weight of 505.5 pounds. Its footpegs are set slightly forward.

## Classic Style

The cruiser is the type of bike that probably comes the closest to what most people think of when they visualize the "classic motorcycle" look. Although motorcycle manufacturers who make cruisers continually refine the style of their bikes with their own engineering ideas, the look of these motorcycles is essentially based on Harley-Davidson or Indian motorcycles, the classic American bikes that became popular from the 1940s through the 1960s. Just about every well-known motorcycling movie and TV show ever made, from *The Wild One* to *Easy Rider* to *Then Came Bronson* to *The Wild Hogs*, has used these types of motorcycles. The look is part of the American psyche, and a lot of riders over forty see riding a bike of this type as the quintessential American motorcycling experience.

a bike with secured storage capacity of some kind is very worthwhile and a great convenience, if only to carry cell phones and other personal items.

*A caution about cruisers*: Think twice about buying a model with what are usually referred to as forward-mounted controls. Commonly used on certain cruiser models, this is a foot-control configuration in which the shift and braking mechanisms are placed far forward on the bike, so the rider sits in a much more elongated position with legs almost straight out in front, and with a foot position operating the shift and brake controls in an almost vertical orientation as it relates to the foot-rest (footpeg) location.

Although taller riders may not find this setup uncomfortable, I caution against buying a bike with this configuration, because the riding position is severe (especially for shorter riders) and makes balancing and controlling a bike

more difficult. Holding your legs and feet in this position often requires more effort to keep your feet on the footpegs, putting increased pressure on your lower back. With this setup, riders often have no other place to rest their feet, and the added strain on the tailbone is uncomfortable—not at all suited to long-distance travel.

In my experience, motorcycles are the easiest to control and generally more comfortable when the shift and brake mechanisms are positioned below the knees and under the feet. When looking for the optimum cruiser riding position, think straight-backed chair or easy chair rather than recliner.

### Standard Advantages
### By Walt Fulton

Standard motorcycles offer a comfortable riding position with foot controls located below the rider and a handlebar height positioned so that the rider does not have to lean forward, which places the shoulders and back in a more natural position.

The Suzuki TU250X is a lightweight standard, a good entry-level bike. A bigger detuned standard can be a good first bike, depending on what a rider can handle.

My first bike was a middleweight cruiser, a Suzuki Intruder 800cc. I bought a used bike for several reasons, one of them being the lower cash outlay.

Standard bikes come in many different configurations and many different sizes, so a good fit can usually be found for most riders.

One very important factor to consider when purchasing any bike is engine size or displacement, and standard motorcycles are no exception. Standards offer a wide variety in levels of engine horsepower, with engine sizes that range from 250cc to 1200cc, and some are very powerful. If you're interested in standard-style motorcycles, as a novice or returning rider, consider a standard that has sufficient power to perform adequately in any street-riding situation, from stop-and-go traffic to riding on the highway, but *not* so much power that the level of performance significantly exceeds your beginning skills as a rider, certainly nothing above the 800cc range.

These bikes appeal to both novice and seasoned riders and are one of the most popular styles of motorcycles on the road. They offer good visibility, a comfortable riding position, a reasonable selection of accessories from saddlebags to windshields, and excellent handling. The versatility, low investment cost, and relatively light weight make this class of motorcycle a good candidate for everything from commuting to touring. (See First Bikes for Women, pages 40–41, for further discussion.)

## Advantages of a Used Bike

I strongly advise new and returning riders not to buy a too-big, high-priced, or brand-new motorcycle as a first purchase. Consider that although you may be a very experienced automobile driver, you are not an experienced motorcyclist, and there is a big difference. There are many motorcycle skills to master, and there is a learning curve to ride up before you begin to get past some of the accidents that are more likely to happen when you're new or just returning to riding. These include dropping the bike and having the bike fall off the kickstand when you forget to put it in gear while parked. As you will come to find out, getting even minor damage repaired on a motorcycle can be an expensive proposition.

Starting out with a reasonably sized, less costly used bike is simply a way to avoid repair expenses associated with inexperience. When I returned to riding, my first motorcycle was a midsize Japanese cruiser. It was a used model, only a few years old, with fewer than 4,000 miles on the odometer, and I

purchased it for about $3,600. Because motorcycles are usually not ridden as primary transportation, they frequently have both low mileage and reasonable price tags when they are resold.

I bought the Japanese cruiser because the bike was physically small enough for me to comfortably handle. Its size and weight (a 61.2-inch wheelbase at 526 pounds) were not significantly greater than those of many bikes at half the displacement, but it had an engine size large enough for me to comfortably maintain highway speeds and have no difficulty keeping pace with traffic.

The motorcycle was in fine shape when I purchased it, and just as important, the purchase price was very reasonable, keeping my initial financial investment in line with the experience level of a

## Streetmasters Advice from *Nancy Foote*

# First Bikes for Women

When I took up riding more than twenty-five years ago, I began with a small bike (a 180cc Honda TwinStar). After a year, I moved on to a 550 Kawasaki Spectre, a standard-type motorcycle. Sure, I had to buy another bike, but because I started small, I had good experiences, stayed on two wheels, and rode a lot. Too many women give up riding because they end up with a bike whose size intimidates them. I try to steer women to the smaller, standard-type bikes, with the footpegs under the rider for greater control and a seat height right for them. In fact, everything on the bike should be an easy reach.

As for engine size, I suggest that a beginner not start on anything bigger than a 600 (or 650 twin). When I say 600, I am referring to the

"detuned"-type bikes, such as the many 600 standards, not the full-on sportbikes. The bike manufacturers aren't producing a large selection of smaller bikes these days, but you can find an assortment of sizes in used bikes. Below are some of my used-bike suggestions for women. (I have included one mild-mannered bike in the 790cc to 865cc range.)

### In the 250–550cc range

■ The Kawasaki 250 Ninja and Honda CBR250R are nice and light, although the seat heights can be a little tall for shorter gals. The Ninja has been around for more than twenty years, so many used bikes can be found. By contrast, the CBR250R (*shown opposite*) is a new addition to the Honda lineup, so used ones may be harder to find.

■ The Honda CB-1 (400cc) is a good starter bike—if you can locate one. This motorcycle has become somewhat of a cult favorite (Honda only brought it to the United States for two years, 1989 and 1990).

■ The Kawasaki EX500 and Suzuki GS500 are good starter bikes.

### In the 600–865cc range

■ The BMW is going after more of the female market with the G650GS models that come with different seat heights. They are pricey when new, but they've been out awhile, so used ones can be found.

■ The Suzuki SV650 is a good choice, but go with the unfaired model because there's less bodywork to damage in the almost inevitable "parking lot tipover" many beginners experience.

beginner or returning rider. Motorcycles of this type and in this price range are plentiful in the marketplace and are typically very reliable. I eventually added traveling accessories to this motorcycle and used it for touring vacations.

## Comfortable Fit

Resist the temptation to buy a motorcycle strictly on looks. Although I began this chapter by talking about the image of your ideal bike, I want to reemphasize here that appearance must be balanced with practical considerations. The most important is proper fit.

If you want something that you can ride for a long afternoon and enjoy every mile, you must buy a bike that is a comfortable fit for your body. This is probably the most frequently overlooked factor in the purchase of a first motorcycle. A motorcycle does not have a ten-way adjustable seat with lumbar support. Only a very few bikes offer even minimal amount of seat, handlebar, and floorboard adjustment.

Positional relationships between the seat, handlebars, and feet position are likely to be the way they are going to be for as long as you own the bike, unless you want to spend a considerable amount of money to change these items from stock. The best option for the purchaser is to buy the bike he or she feels the most comfortable sitting on.

■ The Kawasaki Ninja 650R is a nice mild-mannered bike

■ The Triumph Bonneville, 790cc to 865cc, is a bit larger in displacement, but it is also a mild-mannered bike and does many things well.

There's no downside to buying a smaller motorcycle to begin riding. Lighter and smaller bikes are more agile, easier to maneuver, less imposing, and more likely to be ridden—all good points to consider before you go out to purchase your first motorcycle.

If you're worried about reselling that first bike, don't be: there is always another new rider needing a smaller motorcycle.

At the 2010–2011 Progressive International Motorcycle Shows' stop in Seattle, Washington, attendees get a feel for various bikes, check out new gear, and generally immerse themselves in all things motorcycling.

## Streetmasters Advice from *Walt Fulton*

# Wrong Bike/Bad Technique

At Streetmasters where we teach advanced cornering for street riders, we often work with riders who have control issues and don't know why. We've found that most problems are due to improper bike fit, poor technique, or both.

Often, poor technique may be the result of poor motorcycle fit. Sometimes these bikes have controls the riders can't physically fit, such as a handlebar that's too tall or too wide. A simple task such as making a U-turn can cause a major problem for a rider who can't reach the handlebar when it's turned to full lock.

If you're having a problem negotiating a corner in your lane of travel, it may be because you're riding a motorcycle that is too massive for you (an inexperienced rider) to handle.

Judge this carefully. Are the handlebars a comfortable reach? Are they too far forward or too far back? Is the position of the foot controls comfortable, and is there any strain on your body to reach the controls? Is the bike's weight and height comfortable for you, and can you put your feet comfortably on the ground?

Realize that any discomfort you feel while simply sitting on the motorcycle will be magnified when you are actually operating the bike on the road. Many motorcycles have gone unridden simply because they gave their owners a backache after several hours of riding. (For further discussion, see Wrong Bike/Bad Technique on the opposite page.)

## Where to Buy the Bike

So where do you buy your first bike? Your options basically come down to either a dealership or a private seller. If you're looking for a new bike, of course, you'll go to a dealership. For used bikes, you can go to a dealership or find a private seller.

Dealerships aren't difficult to locate, but ask motorcycling friends or former instructors for suggestions on specific dealerships to visit. Some of the dealerships have better customer service than others do. You can locate private sellers through many outlets, including online services such as eBay and Craigslist, auctions, and local newspapers. In order

Bikes are lined up at a motorcycle dealership, which is a great place to try sitting on bikes of different types and sizes . You can go here to buy a new or used bike.

to get an idea of what you should be paying for a specific motorcycle, you can consult some of the same sources that are available to those who are buying automobiles.

Two of these sources are NADAguides.com (the online version of the printed National Automobile Dealers Association Appraisal Guides) and www.kbb .com/othervehicles (the online location of the *Kelley Blue Book*). These two sources have price guides for both new and used motorcycles. So once you have a good idea of which motorcycle you want, you can determine approximately what you should pay for that bike by using these sources. Never go shopping without finding out this information; you'll be at a distinct disadvantage.

## Dealerships

As mentioned earlier, dealerships and motorcycle shows are great places to look at and get the feel of different bikes. When it comes to buying, however, a motorcycle show is not the place to go. If you go to a dealership to buy a used bike, understand that just

### Streetmasters Advice from *Walt Fulton*

# Be Thorough When Buying

When buying a new motorcycle, realize that—as with an automobile—as soon as you sign your name to the sales paperwork, the price of the bike has depreciated at least $1,000. If you take into account incentives, discounts, low interest rates, warranties, other perks, and the fact that you are getting a brand-new motorcycle, then the depreciation may not be a concern. For most buyers, however, it may be more prudent, financially, to consider a used motorcycle for a first bike.

Often, the excitement of your very first motorcycle purchase may get in the way of a thorough vehicle inspection. This may not be so detrimental with a new bike that's under warranty, but it can be disastrous with a used bike. Don't short-cut this important step when you want to go used-bike shopping. If you arrive at the dealership or private party's residence with a written checklist, you won't overlook important points. Consider the following list when looking for a used motorcycle.

**Overall condition**: From a distance, look for signs of damage, such as bent bars and flaws in the paint that may be the result of crash repair. Closer up, check the footpegs, mirrors, and levers. Are they bent or scraped? Depending on the type of bike, scraped footpeg feelers or floorboards may be a clue about how hard the bike was used by the previous owner.

**Clutch cable**: If the clutch is cable operated, look at the cable adjustment and condition of the cable. Is the adjuster screwed all the way out? Is the cable kinked? Can you squeeze and release the lever smoothly? If

A rider checks over a motorcycle. Inspect a bike thoroughly before buying.

as in an automobile purchase, the price there may be higher than elsewhere, but it may still be negotiable.

If (and that is a big if) the dealership took the time to completely get the bike up to top condition, it might be worth paying a bit more. In addition, if you aren't handy with tools or have no interest in maintaining a bike yourself, then buying from a dealer may be the best way to go. By purchasing from a dealership, you can establish a relationship with a service department specializing in motorcycles and set up a routine bike-maintenance schedule.

## Private Sellers

Frequently, the best deals on any purchase will be available through private sellers. The reasons are obvious—no overhead, more ability to negotiate, and no taxes at the time of sale. There are many reasons an owner may want to sell a bike as quickly as possible, including wanting a newer, larger, or different style of bike; undergoing a change in financial status; and losing interest in riding (yes, it happens). Whatever the reason, it means outlay of cash for you.

the clutch is hydraulic, you may not be able to feel anything unusual, but ask where the slave cylinder is located and inspect for leaks. Note the color of the fluid in the reservoir: a light color is good; a dark color indicates contaminants. The latter means the clutch reservoir needs to be flushed out and refilled with fresh fluid, and it might be an indicator of lack of routine maintenance.

**Throttle cable**: Most likely there will be two cables, one to open the throttle and one to close it. Check the adjustment and operation by slowly opening and closing the throttle. It should be smooth. Fully open the throttle and release the grip. Does it snap closed (good) or does it stick open (bad)?

**Brakes**: Most current motorcycles are fitted with disc brakes, front and rear. There are three items that you should be aware of here: 1) Rotors—look at the rotor condition for hot spots (areas of discoloration) and excessive wear. 2) Brake pads—a visual inspection will give you an idea of how far the pads are

worn. Typically, when the brake material reaches between 1mm and 1.5mm, it's time to replace the pads as a pair. 3) Brake fluid—be sure to inspect the color of the brake fluid. Light is good; dark is bad.

**Forks and shocks**: Look for nicks in the front fork tubes. These could damage the seal and cause the fork oil to leak out. Can you compress the forks and shocks, and do they move smoothly through their compression and rebound stroke? With the handlebar centered, is the front wheel pointing straight ahead? If not, take a look at the fork stops to see if they have been damaged by the fork being forced to one side or the other. Damage here may be the result of a crash.

**Steering bearings**: Checking these may be a two-person job, one that can be easily done if the bike is fitted with a center stand. Raise the front wheel off the ground and turn the bars full lock to the left and then right. Does the steering assembly turn smoothly, or do you feel it index, or catch, as

it is rotated? A catch indicates damaged bearing races. With the front wheel off the ground, grasp the lower portion of the forks and try to pull them to you and then push them away from you. Do you feel any back and forth movement? Any play is bad, a sign that adjustments or repairs are needed.

**Tires**: Motorcycle tires can be a major expense, so make certain that there are plenty of miles left in the tires when you purchase a used bike. If the tread is down to the wear bars (typically $\frac{1}{32}$ inch of tread left), it's time to replace the tire(s). If the tires are worn flat in the center, you can figure that the bike was used primarily for straight-line riding. These, too, need to be replaced regardless of remaining tread, as these squared-off tires will not allow you to corner very well. In addition, if you are looking at an older used bike, check the date of manufacture molded in the sidewall. Any tire more than several years old should be replaced immediately.

The well-known auction site eBay is one place to check for used motorcycles, but try to find sellers within driving distances so you can see the bikes in person.

>>> A Rider's Tale

# Ed's Story: Let Wishes Be . . . Motorcycles

Horses are a lot of work, as I found out. My dad was a semiprofessional team roper and a rodeo fanatic, so it was natural for me to want a horse. After a couple of years of riding and the constant care a horse demands, though, I was looking for something else. One day, I noticed a derelict three-cylinder motorcycle parked in a storage shed, and that started me dreaming about riding a motorcycle.

In 1969, my parents must have gotten the idea that my mind was set on riding a motorcycle. On Christmas morning that year, I found a new 1970 Yamaha 50cc motorcycle, er, scooter, under the tree. Because I was too young to ride on the road, I spent countless miles and hours riding the Yamaha like it was a dirt bike until it was

nearly destroyed. As time passed, I got progressively larger bikes: a Yamaha 90, a Honda XL125, and a 1976 Honda CR250R motocrosser, my first racing bike.

It was a lean, mean, fast, scream-ing, racing machine that I rode ev-ery chance I got and with which I eventually started racing. Unfortu-nately, after two years of racing, I found myself broke. Buying spark plugs, pistons, rings, replacement gears, and, of course, tires had ex-hausted my supply of summer-work savings. I sold the bike in 1978 and walked away from motorcycling.

In 1980, my professional life be-gan. I became a flight instructor and a few years later an air-traffic controller. The extensive training in-volved with becoming an air-traffic

controller and a flight instructor de-pleted all extra funds, and I didn't have time to pursue motorcycles anymore. I never lost the love for riding, just the time and money.

Not until late 2000 did I get the motorcycle bug again. I don't re-member exactly why then. It may have been a magazine article that rekindled my interest, or just sudden memories of my early years on two wheels, but I found myself hooked just as I had been in 1967. My search landed me a 2001 Kawasaki KLR650. I didn't know anything about the Mo-torcycle Safety Foundation and its riding classes so I went to the DMV, got the riding permit, and picked up the *California Motorcycle Manual*. I read it, practiced a lot, followed the rules, and took the test.

There are several easy-to-access places to look for private sales, among them TraderOnline (www .traderonline.com), Craigslist, and the well-known auction site eBay. TraderOnline and Craigslist will allow you to limit searches to cities or specific distances from your zip code, and this will give you the opportunity to contact the seller and arrange to see and inspect the motorcycle prior to any purchase. If you can, take a mechanic friend or a more knowledgeable rider along to help check out the bike. Ask the owner to show you the bike's maintenance records, and be prepared to ask lots and lots of questions.

EBay is also a viable source for purchases, but I would discourage buying any bike on the basis of ads or pictures on the Internet.

Unless a seller makes a point of giving a full description of a bike, the typically small photograph or series of small photographs used in an eBay description can hide general finish issues, scratches, old or worn tires, or poor general condition. EBay sellers also can live anywhere in the country, which often makes the logistics of a purchase difficult. Bear mind, too, that with eBay, as with any Internet site, buying and selling scams can be a problem.

Don't discount the eBay option, however. I found my last motorcycle on it. Fortunately, the seller happened to live in a city less than seventy miles away, which meant I could easily drive there to have a look at the bike and make the purchase directly.

That KLR turned out to be a match made in heaven. It was exactly the kind of bike for me, and since getting the KLR, I've ridden it all over the southwestern California desert and coastal areas, not to mention taking trips on it to Moab, Utah, and Death Valley, California, over the last ten years. The motorcycle is still going strong.

Ed Snow (posing here without his usual riding gear) on his FJR1300

In 2009, I decided to expand my horizons and buy a street motorcycle. As with the KLR, I researched many bikes before settling on a new 2009 Yamaha FJR1300. The FJR is sporty, has lots of power, is smooth and comfortable, and has room to pack for a couple of weeks on the road. I've had many adventures and good times riding solo and with some large groups all over Southern California.

I am fifty years old, with two bikes in my garage and many, many miles to ride ahead of me. I am looking forward to each and every one of them!

# CHAPTER 3

# GETTING YOUR BIKE UP TO SPEED

>>> You've got your license, you've got your bike (and have been practicing your riding techniques), your spirits are soaring, and you feel ready to venture farther afield. But before you "head out on the highway," make sure that your motorcycle is completely roadworthy. The last thing you want is to be stuck on the side of the highway because you didn't bring your bike up to top mechanical condition before taking it on a longer ride or tour. This step is especially important if you bought a used bike.

When buying a used bike from a private owner, ask for any service records on the bike so you can check the maintenance history. Take the bike to a good dealership that does service on your make of motorcycle, and ask that it be checked for any and all items that may not have been maintained on the bike.

Have the mechanic inspect the entire bike for any other services you might need. These could include changing the oil (fork oil, as well), replacing worn brake pads, checking the battery and charging system, and changing brake and clutch reservoir fluids (for bikes with a hydraulic clutch), as well as changing the final drive gear lubricant on a shaft-drive bike and the coolant in a liquid-cooled bike.

If the bike has a chain drive (*left*), have the chain and sprockets closely inspected as well. As time goes on, you may learn to perform many of these maintenance tasks yourself, as most are fairly simple procedures. The first time, however, pay a reputable mechanic to do it so he or she can spot problems that you may not be aware of. The peace of mind is worth the money. If you are buying a used bike from a dealership and think the bike may not have been serviced recently, discuss bringing the servicing up to date as part of the purchase, or ask for maintenance records to show what has or hasn't been done.

There are certain maintenance items and additional equipment that should be included with the bike when it is purchased, and others that you should plan to add after buying a motorcycle. Some of these are simple, common sense items; others are more major purchases.

## A Tool Kit

**M**ost motorcycles come with a basic tool kit; check to see that it is included when you purchase a bike. To be honest, most tools included in such a kit are fairly generic, and many are cheaply made. The few that are specifically sized to the bike are worth keeping (for example, open-end wrenches, Allen wrenches, and wheel-axle wrenches). Typically, I will replace a few included items with tools of better quality (such as screwdrivers and a small socket set) and supplement the tool kit with cable ties, electrical tape, a bright LED flashlight, and small bungee cords—not usually included in a kit but useful for minor repairs on the road.

A socket set, cable ties, a flashlight, and several bungee cords form part of my bike tool kit.

## Owners and Service Manuals

If a motorcycle you've purchased does not have the original owner's manual, order one from the bike's manufacturer. You may also find one on websites such as eBay. Various websites offer links to downloadable manuals, but you'll have to do some searching to find the one you want. Fees are sometimes involved, so be sure to check the terms of use before downloading.

The owner's manual has lots of specific information about your make and model—control adjustments, fuses and the battery, seat removal, maintenance tasks, and so on. Consider purchasing a service manual for the bike as well. A generic service manual will usually cover several similar models, and while you may not use the information on engine and transmission rebuilding, the manual is valuable if you plan to perform routine maintenance on the bike. A service manual will include simple maintenance procedures such as changing the oil and replacing the air filter, as well as changing brake pads, flushing and refilling fluids, and changing instrument indicator bulbs, headlight(s), taillights, and brake lights.

## Engine Protector Bars (Case Guards)

Engine protectors, also called case guards, are tubular steel bars (often chromed) that attach at the front of the frame and below the gas tank and are designed to prevent damage if the bike falls. Leaving the bike in neutral with the kickstand down on even a slight incline, or where the pavement is significantly higher on one side of the bike than the other, can result in a tip-over—the kind of mishap more likely to happen to an inexperienced rider. Here, engine protector bars will be well worth the investment; without them,

The Victory Cross Country comes with engine protector bars, but you will probably have to add them to smaller and less expensive motorcycles.

# American Motorcyclist Association

Join the American Motorcyclist Association (AMA), and in addition to being part of a great organization that supports motorcyclists and motorcycling, you'll enjoy several benefits: getting riding gear at reduced prices at many motorcycling retail outlets and Internet sites, getting reduced rates on hotel rooms (and rental cars, should you need one), and having the option to add roadside assistance and towing to your membership. I have been riding fifteen years and have only needed this service twice, but it was more than a convenience to have—it made the difficult situation of having a mechanical failure on the road much easier to deal with.

Membership in the AMA also includes a subscription to *American Motorcyclist* magazine, which through its motorcycling advocacy group keeps you informed about political issues governing motorcycling. Undoubtedly, the most important aspect of the AMA is its legislative activities; the AMA has been involved in lobbying for motorcyclists' rights since 1924. With more than 300,000 members, the AMA is the largest nationwide traveling and advocacy organization for motorcycle riders, and it's an organization worth supporting. You can find information on the AMA at www.ama-cycle.org.

even a minor fall can do fairly serious cosmetic damage that will cost a pretty penny to repair. In addition, waiting for parts and repairs can sometimes take weeks and can put your bike out of commission for several months of the riding season.

Engine protector bars should be wide enough to keep the motorcycle's fuel tank well off the ground and to minimize damage to the hand and foot controls and side mirrors. These bars are a relatively inexpensive safeguard for your investment. They also offer a place to locate highway pegs, which are supplementary foot rests that allow a change of riding position and a stretch of the legs when you are on the bike for a long day. In a worst-case scenario, such as a sliding crash, they do offer some protection to the legs and hips.

Motorcycles are not usually sold with engine protector bars, but many owners add them, particularly to cruisers, so used bikes traded in at dealerships often have the bars. If this aftermarket item has not been added to a bike that you want to buy, I highly recommend that you purchase it.

The tread on this tire looks level with the wear bar (rectangular block circled in red), indicating that this tire need to be replaced immediately.

## »» A Rider's Tale
# Susan's Story: Personalizing the Ride

As a girl, I began riding minibikes and dirt bikes with my brothers, so all it took was a little encouragement from my first husband, who dearly loved riding, to get my first street bike. He helped me to pick out a bike that would be a good starter bike, a Kawasaki 440 LTD, and henceforth I became a pilot instead of a passenger.

I loved the feeling of the wind whipping around me, the smells, the cool mornings, the warmth of catching a low thermal, the hum of the engine. It was pure pleasure, but when my first husband and I divorced, I stopped riding for several years.

Then I married another motorcycle enthusiast and started riding my own bike again, this time purchasing a 1993 Sportster 883. While I thoroughly enjoyed my Kawasaki 440, it had always felt less stable to me at highway speeds, because its lower weight (406 pounds) made the bike susceptible to crosswinds and buffeting. The greater weight of the Sportster (489 pounds) made the bike feel more solid and stabler to me, and I felt safer and more comfortable riding the larger bike.

After owning the Sportster for a while, I began personalizing it, having the bike lowered to fit my "vertical challenge," installing 4-inch pull-back risers on the handlebars for a more comfortable reach, and adding a small fairing to deflect the wind. Mechanical changes included adding an H-D Screamin' Eagle carburetor kit and air cleaner and having the baffles bored in the stock pipes to give them a deeper rumble and increase the bike's performance. Later on, I added hard-mounted leather bags to make packing for travel a bit easier. The

# Tires and Tire Maintenance

**D**o not neglect your motorcycle tires in any way. Maintaining them is extremely important. Keep them properly inflated (I typically check mine twice a week during riding season), and replace them as soon as you need to. Motorcycle tires are manufactured with softer compounds than those used for automobile tires to give a bike increased traction. Although these compounds offer more stick, they also wear more quickly. Worn tires not only have lower road adhesion but also affect the bike's handling and can lead to a blowout on the road. A blowout while moving at high speed can result in a loss of control and a serious accident.

Susan Kennerly with her
1993 Sportster 883, "a great bike"

883 was a great bike, and I kept it and enjoyed it for ten years.

I carry many fond memories of being a biker chick, stylin' in black leather riding gear. On glorious spring days, when the sky was a cloudless blue and the temperatures in the mid-sixties, I piloted my two wheels through the winding hills of the north Georgia mountains, with the wind in my face and the smell of honeysuckle in the air.

There are no spare tires on motorcycles, and getting a flat on the road is, at best, a great inconvenience. What's more, regular service stations usually do not have the equipment for, or people experienced in, motorcycle-tire repair. Check and maintain your tires regularly.

## Wear Bars and Tire Dates

Motorcycle tires (as well as automotive tires) use what are called wear bars in the tread to indicate tire wear. These are small horizontal bars placed inside the tread (see opposite page) at locations around the tire. You can often locate them by looking for small triangular arrows on the tire's sidewall (*see below*), indicating where the wear bars are placed in the tread. These bars become more apparent as tire wear approaches their level. Tires should be replaced before tread wear reaches the level of the wear bars.

An often-overlooked issue is the age of the tires. Preowned motorcycles sometimes have been infrequently ridden; that means the tires may have been on the bike for many years, possibly since the bike was new. They may look good, but the rubber compounds have become less flexible and the tread more brittle and hardened, thereby reducing traction. Check the date code on the tires, which will show the year of their manufacture. If the code indicates that they are more than three years old, or if there is any doubt about the general condition of the tires, they should be replaced.

The date code can be found on the sidewall of both motorcycle and automotive tires. The date code follows the Department of Transportation (DOT) designation. For tires manufactured after the year 2000, the last four numbers indicate the week and year of manufacture. In the figure shown above, the code "DOT xxxx xxxx 3707" indicates that this tire was manufactured in the thirty-seventh week (September) of 2007. For tires manufactured before 2000, the code ends in three numbers, indicating a two-digit week and a single-digit year of the decade. For example, if the last digits in a pre-2000 code were "507," this would indicate that the tire was manufactured in the fiftieth week (December) of 1997. It's not likely that you'll find a motorcycle that is otherwise roadworthy that has tires manufactured over a decade ago, but obviously, tires this old need to be replaced immediately.

## Tire Repair Kit

An important item to keep with the bike is an emergency tire repair kit. Motorcycles are now often manufactured with wheels that use tubeless tires (rather than spoked wheels, most of which use tubes inside the tires). This wheel and tire option has several advantages, including making the tires more resistant to blowouts. In addition, a leak in a tubeless tire is more easily plugged using a standard tire (plug) repair kit. Compact motorcycle-tire repair kits are made for a fairly straightforward application: repairing a hole caused by a nail or screw in a tubeless tire. The compact kits generally consist of a plug kit and some small $CO_2$ cartridges designed to reinflate a tire.

### Streetmasters Advice from *Walt Fulton*

# Rubber Meets the Road

Use a gauge to check tire pressure on a regular basis.

After riding several blistering laps around the tri-oval at the Las Vegas Motor Speedway, a wannabe racer was asked by a tire engineer what he thought about the tires. He replied, "They're black, round, and made of rubber." Some riders have the same opinion. Check the condition of the tires mounted on the various motorcycles at the next motorcycle event you attend. On many bikes, the tires are worn out in the center or completely worn out and have long outlived their time in this world. (And don't think that filling the cracks in old tires with black shoe polish, as the movie version of motorcyclist Burt Munro did in the film *The World's Fastest Indian*, is going to fix anything.) Tire technology has made huge advancements over the past decade. Tires last longer, stick to the ground better, and work better in wet weather. You have a choice of compounds from gum eraser soft to rock hard, and you can even buy race tires and slicks approved by the DOT.

A common factor found in motorcycle accidents is underinflated tires. This comes under the heading of "out of sight, out of mind." You may not notice this underinflation until you need to make an aggressive stop, perform an evasive maneuver, or navigate a tight corner—just when you need everything working at its optimum level! Checking tire pressure regularly, as well as inspecting the tread for wear and foreign objects, is an inexpensive form of insurance. Make it part of your pre-ride check every time you ride. (For further discussion, see Are You Ready to Ride? on pages 56–57.)

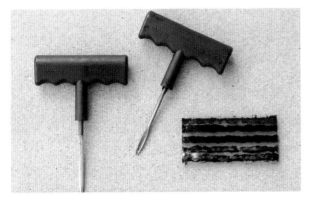

Part of a motorcycle-tire repair kit

specifically for motorcycle tires, and if you have a can of this product on hand when you have a flat, of course you're going to use it. And while automotive tire sealants are not recommended for motorcycle use, if a can of automotive tire sealant and inflator is all that's available, using it (literally) as a stopgap method still probably makes sense, if only to get you to a location where the tire can be repaired. Bear in mind, however, that there is no guarantee that such sealants will work, as the location and nature of the puncture affect the performance of these products.

*Warning:* If you use a canned sealant, you *must* remember to tell the person repairing the tire that you have done so, as the propellant used in the product is flammable and therefore explosive in a pressurized tire.

Whether your bike has tubeless tires or tubed ones, any tire repair is only a temporary measure designed to get you home or to a repair shop. Never continue to ride on a repaired tire for longer than absolutely necessary. Motorcycle tires are subject to much greater stresses in normal operation than are automotive tires, which makes repairs much less reliable. In addition, a tire failure will most often result in a difficult control situation. The only way to avoid the possibility of a plugged tire failing again is to replace the tire.

With traditional spoked wheels, which use tubes inside the tire, repairing a leak using a patch kit on the open road is generally not a practical option. Repairing or replacing a tube usually requires removal of the wheel from the chassis and then removal of the tire from the wheel. If the bike does not have a center stand (or some method to keep the bike's weight off the tire that needs repair) and you do not have a set of motorcycle tire irons (tools that most riders do not carry), you will not be able to perform this repair in the field.

However, if your bike has tubed tires, and you get a flat when you are in "the middle of nowhere" and do not have other options to get the tire repaired, you may be able to use a can of tire sealant to seal a leak and reinflate a tire if you remove the source of the puncture. You can also use standard tire repair $CO_2$ cartridges or a small compressor to supplement these products (12-volt-powered compressors sized to fit in motorcycle saddlebags are available through motorcycle outlets, and you may want to consider purchasing one). Understand that tire sealants should only be used in an emergency to reinflate a tire in order to get you to a location where a replacement tube can be installed.

There are tire sealant products designed

Compressor for inflating tires

## Antilock Brakes

**R**iding south after a day riding through the north Georgia foothills, while passing through a small town on a 45-miles-per-hour, two-lane rural highway, I turned my head quickly to the left to look at a road sign. When I looked again at the traffic in front of me, a car making a left-hand turn into a convenience-store parking lot had completely stopped in the lane ahead. I hit the brakes for all I was worth, bringing the bike from the speed limit down to approximately 15 miles per hour in a very short distance, then released the brakes and steered the bike around

the right side of the car on the wide shoulder of the road, avoiding what might have been a serious accident. At the time, I owned a BMW sport-touring motorcycle, which had an antilock braking system (ABS) as standard equipment. To be honest, I don't know if the ABS ever activated, but knowing that wheel lockup would not cause me to crash allowed me to concentrate fully on taking evasive action.

Highly skilled riders have shown that they can stop a motorcycle faster without an antilock brake system. Most riders are not this skilled, however, and would probably not have the presence of mind in an emergency situation to apply the precise amount of force to the front and rear brakes to get the maximum braking, just short of the point at

Honda's CBR250R can be purchased with ABS for an extra charge. At this time, ABS is mostly available for big, high-end bikes, but this is changing.

# Are You Ready to Ride?

Riding is more than throwing your leg over the seat, thumbing the starter button, and heading off on another great adventure. The next time you go for a ride, do yourself a favor by taking a critical look at your pre-ride routine. Are you checking your gear to make sure you have everything you may need and that the various items are in good condition? Even more importantly, are you checking your bike thoroughly to make sure that everything on it is in working order? Performing a pre-ride check every time may seem unnecessary, especially when you are anxious to get out and ride, but doing so is critical for your safety and only takes a few minutes.

You probably learned the procedure for checking your bike in your basic riding course, along with the handy acronym to aid you in remembering the key areas of interest: T-CLOCK.

- **T**: Tires and wheels
- **C**: Controls
- **L**: Lights
- **O**: Oil
- **C**: Chassis
- **K**: Kickstand/center stand

A rider runs through a check on the motorcycle. Run through the T-CLOCK check each time before riding.

**Tires**: Low pressure in your tires can lead to premature tire wear, sluggish handling, increased stopping distances, and a reduction of traction while cornering. Low tire pressure can also cause stability issues. Because motorcycle tires have such stiff sidewalls, even a 10 or 15 psi (pounds per square inch) drop in pressure may not be noticeable. Regularly check for proper inflation and punctures as well as tread depth.

**Controls**: Before each ride, operate all controls to make certain they work smoothly. This is also a good time to glance at the brake pads (front and rear) to make sure that there is ample material on them.

which the tires lose traction. This is especially true of new and returning riders, who are still working on the basics of braking in different situations. Bear in mind, too, that any miscalculation in brake application that causes a traction loss means that the bike must be brought back into control before the rider can take further evasive action, which lessens the amount of time he or she has to avoid an accident. In my opinion, if you are buying a new bike that has ABS as an option, you would be wise to spend the extra money to get it.

## Consider This

At the beginning of 2011, I checked the difference in price for one full-size motorcycle, a Triumph Thunderbird, that offers ABS as an option. The price without ABS is $12,499; with ABS, $13,200. This comes to about $700 dollars, or approximately a 5.6 percent increase in suggested retail price. In the case of other motorcycles with a list price of over $10,000, the cost of adding ABS averaged 7.25 percent over the base cost of the bike. (The typical cost of adding ABS is $500–$1,000.) If you were already planning to spend more than $10,000 for a bike, wouldn't you spend less than 10 percent more for ABS? For me, the answer is a no-brainer.

**Lights**: For visibility and conspicuity, make certain that all lights are functioning. Don't overlook the turn signals, the taillight, and the stoplight.

**Oil**: *O* is not only for engine oil; it's also a reminder to check any fluid you use in your motorcycle, including gasoline and radiator coolant. Oil is the lifeblood of the engine, and on many bikes, checking the oil level is as simple as looking at the sight glass on the side of the engine. On shaft-drive machines, it's not practical to remove the filler plug on the rear drive to check the oil level, so always keep an eye open for oil leaking out of the drive.

**Chassis**: The chassis includes frame, suspension, chain/belt, and fasteners. Thoroughly cleaning your bike will not only help you protect your investment but also help you identify loose fasteners. Today's chains will last for many miles, but they must be kept clean, lubricated, and adjusted. Don't let chain lube build up on the chain, as it collects abrasive grime that destroys the sprockets. If you see the sprocket teeth begin to hook, it's time for a pair of sprockets (front and rear) and a new chain.

**Kickstand**: Would you ever expect a side stand to give out and "let you down"? Sitting on the bike with the side stand down is a surefire way to ruin your day. Stands are designed to hold the weight of the bike and a reasonable amount of added gear—not to support the bike, rider, and passenger. For peace of mind, keep the side stand pivot lubed, and keep an eye on the clevis for cracks or spreading.

In addition to running through a T-CLOCK check before each ride, you can perform a bike check on the wash rack. Not only does cleaning your bike keep it looking nice and improve the resale value, but it also gives you a chance to look at every exposed fastener. The smoother the engine runs, the less trouble you'll have with fasteners coming loose. Even on the smoothest multicylinder bikes, this happens with fasteners. A single-cylinder, large-bore motorcycle has more of a tendency to loosen every nut and bolt that's not safety wired or coated with a thread-locking compound.

A visual inspection is the first step to assuring yourself that all of the fasteners are snug and that you aren't ready to lose the front-axle pinch bolts or some other strategic fastener. Cleaning also removes *smashed* (technical term) bugs that can damage your paint.

Remember that the outcome of any ride depends on the condition of your motorcycle. It's your responsibility to make sure that your bike is in the best condition possible before you leave home.

# CHAPTER 4

# FINDING THE RIGHT GEAR

>>> The bike isn't all that needs to be outfitted properly for the road; you have to gear up as well. You'll find that appropriate and good-quality riding gear will vastly increase your comfort level while you're out on the road, especially when you're caught in bad weather. The right helmet, clothing, boots, and gloves can also save your skin—literally.

When taking on any new sport or hobby—whether that be motorcycling, skiing, or even woodworking—you should consider not only the possibilities for enjoyment and personal achievement and growth but also the logical steps to minimize the possibility of injury. In motorcycling, those steps include getting and wearing good-quality protective gear. Many riding instructors teach their students the acronym ATGATT—all the gear, all the time.

## Where to Shop

Cost for these items varies from reasonable to very expensive. As with most things, paying the highest prices does not always get you the best stuff, so do some comparison shopping for price and quality before you shell out your hard-earned bucks. You can check out the gear at motorcycle dealerships, which usually carry all of the basic items you will need, as well as at retail stores that sell motorcycling gear primarily. Because their focus is on selling motorcycling products, not motorcycles, these retail stores often have prices on gear that are more competitive than those at the dealerships and have quality items on their clearance racks. Motorcycling retail stores can usually be found in most cities and many smaller towns.

Gear consignment shops such as Yellow Devil Gear Exchange (*above*), in Long Beach, California, are good places to get secondhand gear for lower prices.

There are many online sites for vendors of this gear (a simple Internet search will probably turn up quite a few). Sign up to get on the mailing lists of these companies to receive printed sales circulars and magazines selling everything motorcycling. Another venue, mentioned in chapter 2, is the motorcycle show. Depending on the show and the venue, you can look over the latest bikes and gear, attend seminars on riding techniques and bike maintenance, see classic motorcycle movies, and watch jaw-dropping stunt shows. That's particularly true at the annual Progressive International Motorcycle Shows (http://www.motorcycleshows.com), which visit twelve metropolitan areas across the country from November to March. You can attend smaller local motorcycle shows as well. These shows are usually held in municipal auditoriums and similar venues and are great places to buy not only traveling gear but also hard-to-find convenience items specific to motorcycling.

At different shows over the years, I have purchased leather riding gear; small, handlebar-mounted, battery-powered clocks; heated clothing accessories; and rain boot covers. I even took in a Total Control Advanced Riding Clinic seminar given for free at one of the Progressive International Motorcycle Shows. Large and small motorcycle shows alike can be as much fun as they are informative and educational.

Consignment shops specializing in motorcycle gear are another source to check into. You can get some good deals on secondhand gear. Because these specialty consignment shops aren't numerous, however, you may not be able to find one in your area. Try doing an online search for "consignment shops motorcycle gear" or something similar. A few of these shops have websites with pictures and descriptions of their inventory.

Incidentally, don't overlook nontraditional sources for clothing that will work in a motorcycling environment. Years ago, I purchased a down-filled, bib-overall-style ski suit that works very well for cold-weather riding; it can be used over protective clothing. I found the suit on the sales rack of a local sporting goods store for $19.95. I still use the suit over a decade later, and it keeps me very comfortable when I am out riding in temperatures as low as 40 degrees.

More recently, I purchased sports-style undergarments made of polyester that pull moisture away from the skin (silk does this, as well), which keeps a rider drier than cotton. This translates into being cooler in hot weather and being warmer in cool weather.

## Helmets

Not everyone likes the idea of wearing a motorcycle helmet or appreciates being told that he or she has to do so, which is reflected in the fact that fewer than half of the states require all riders to wear one. Yet much greater risks for serious head injury are associated with motorcycling than with driving a car, and there's no denying that wearing a helmet does significantly lower those risks.

Several studies—including, of course, the Hurt Report—support the effectiveness of wearing a helmet in the prevention of serious injury and death in an accident. Here are some of findings from the Hurt Report on the helmet issue:

Participants at a rally, waiting for the procession to start, display a range of (or lack of) head gear, but being fully helmeted when riding is the best and safest option.

- Voluntary safety helmet use by those accident-involved motorcycle riders was lowest for untrained, uneducated, young motorcycle riders on hot days and short trips.
- The most deadly injuries to the accident victims were injuries to the chest and head.
- The use of the safety helmet is the single most critical factor in the prevention or reduction of head injury.
- Helmeted riders and passengers showed significantly lower rates of head and neck injury for all types of injury, at all levels of injury severity.
- The increased coverage of the full facial coverage helmet increases protection and significantly reduces face injuries.

And from the article "Motorcycle Accident Statistics" published on webBikeWorld.com:

Helmet usage made a significant difference in the survivability of motorcycle accidents. The NHTSA report estimated that helmets were 37 percent effective in preventing fatalities, and that helmets saved the lives of 1,316 motorcyclists in 2004, but that the lives of 671 motorcyclists who died could have been saved if they had been wearing helmets. Nationwide, 44 percent of motorcyclists involved in fatal accidents were not wearing helmets.

In the states where wearing a helmet is optional, people must decide for themselves if they want to use the protection. When I got back on a motorcycle, I decided I would never ride without a helmet, regardless of a particular state's laws. Let's face it, although motorcycling is one of the most enjoyable pastimes

## Tips on Gear from *GearChic*

# Make Sure Your Gear Fits

Joanne Donn, the founder of GearChic.com, says her mission is "to provide reviews, tips, and insights on all things related to what you (men and women) should be wearing while riding your motorcycle or scooter. If you're just starting out and don't know what to wear, how it should fit, or where to get it, I'll do my best to point you in the right direction." She also works part time as an MSF instructor and as an apparel specialist at a motorcycle dealership in San Francisco.

## Shopping Tips

Here are GearChic's five rules to keep in mind when gear shopping.

**Rule #1: Fit, then budget.**

■ There are many reasons, from the materials used to where it's manufactured to the overall quality, why one jacket (or any other piece of gear) costs more than another. More often than not, the key difference is fit. Well-fitting gear offers greater safety, and well-fitting gear is frequently more expensive. When you're shopping around, don't let the price tag keep you from trying something on. What's most important to first find something that fits.

■ When you end up finding the perfect jacket in terms of fit, features, and protection, it may very well exceed your budget. At this point, you may change your mind about how much you are willing to spend. If you just can't spend more than you originally budgeted, at least you know what style of jacket fits and can try to find a less expensive version.

**Rule #2: Always judge proper fit while sitting on a motorcycle in a riding position.**

■ A business suit or casual clothes are not designed to fit a great deal differently when you're sitting than you're standing. Motorcycle gear, by contrast, is designed to be far more comfortable in a riding position than in a standing position. In fact, if you're wearing gear that fits properly, you'll notice that it feels more uncomfortable when you stand up with your arms at your sides than it does when you're sitting on the bike, with arms outstretched, hands on the grips.

■ It is normal for a jacket to feel somewhat uncomfortable (as if there's not enough material) when you push your shoulders back or raise your hands above your head. The manufacturer designed the jacket to be more comfortable in the riding position, because that is the position you will be in most of the time that you are wearing the jacket.

**Rule #3: If it's too comfortable, it's probably too big.**

■ Many of us prefer to buy regular clothing that is loose and comfortable. We want something easy to pull on and pull off. Sometimes we just don't like the fitted look or the tight feel of clothing.

■ With motorcycle gear, the fit and sizing work hand in hand with the protective nature of the gear. Body armor is set to fit over your shoulders, elbows, hips, and knees. If the gear is too large, then the protective panels won't be positioned properly over those areas and will not protect them in an accident.

■ Another problem with an oversize jacket or an oversize pair of pants is the gear's inability to provide proper insulation. Too much space between your body and your gear means you're likely to get wind up your back, up your sleeves, down your chest, or up your pant legs.

**Rule #4: Try on everything until you find the right fit.**

■ It is crucial that you find the riding gear that matches your body type. The right fit will make for a far more comfortable ride, and comfort means you'll be more likely to wear the gear, all the time.

■ Ladies, finding gear that fits can be a more difficult venture for you than for men. We have curves where men don't, and this can definitely make things difficult when we're trying to find well-fitting gear. Gear for women has come a long way and there are more options than ever before, but we still have fewer choices than men do, so it may take you longer to find something that feels right.

▪ More often than not, a manufacturer will stick to a similar body type to model all its lines after, so keep trying gear on until you find a company/style that matches your type as closely as possible. Gear varies greatly from company to company in terms of sizing and cuts.

**Rule #5**: **Leather should always start out snug so it can stretch and break in comfortably.**

▪ If you are trying on a new leather jacket or a new pair of leather gloves, or pants, keep in mind that they're going to stretch as you break them in. You want leather gear to be a little snug when you buy it.

▪ Ask yourself: "If these pants [for example] could be a bit bigger, but not a full size bigger, would they be perfect?" If you answer yes, then they just need time to break in.

▪ Keep in mind that different types of hides may fit and break in differently. Kangaroo, for instance, stretches out right away and tends to require less break-in time than does cow. (Synthetic leather breaks in more quickly than does real leather—and breaks down more quickly as well!)

### Head to Toe

Here are GearChic's tips on getting the right fit for basic gear.

**Helmets**: Fit is determined by head shape, not cheek fit. Measure your head (from the back to front: just above the ears to just above the eyebrows) so you know about what size to start with. Be aware, though, that helmet sizes and shapes do vary among manufacturers.

"Chipmunk cheeks" (pads inside the helmet that press against your cheeks) are normal; the cheek pads will break in. Wear the helmet in the store for fifteen minutes or so to see if pressure points develop. If they do or you have any doubts about the fit, keep looking.

**Jackets**: When you try on a jacket, close all zippers, snaps, and buttons. If you have layers for different seasons, try the jacket on without the lining and with multiple layers. Choose the jacket for the layers you'll wear the most; all protective pieces—over shoulder, elbow, and back, should fall in the right places.

The right base layers (whether are included or are bought separately) can make or break your jacket as well as your pants when it comes to extreme cold or hot weather or when you're wearing leather.

**Gloves**: For the best protection, look for a gauntlet, knuckle armor, and reinforced and double-stitched palms. Form the letter *C* with your hands, then check the fit, or better yet, walk over to a bike and place your hands on the handlebar grips. Try on the gloves with your jacket on to make sure that the sleeves fit comfortably inside the gauntlet.

**Pants**: Pants should be a little too long when you're standing so they will fit properly when you are in a riding position. Look for knee and hip protection and added layers for your buttocks. Pants that have zippers up the side from the ankle to past the knee are overpants and are meant to be worn over your street clothes. They can be slipped on and off over your boots. Sealed zippers and Velcro over the pockets indicate a waterproof pair of pants.

**Boots**: Motorcycle boots will provide more traction than regular street boots will. Find a pair that has extra support in around the ankles for more stability and give confidence you need to support the weight of the bike. Look for armor at the impact points: toes, heels, shins, and ankle bones.

Your boots have two jobs. First, they should stay on your feet. Street shoes can come off your feet way too easily when you are riding. Riding boots will have secure features—Velcro, buckles, and zippers—to make sure that they don't go anywhere without your permission. Second, the boots should keep your feet from being crushed by your motorcycle or damaged in any situation in which they are caught between the bike and an object. Looking for armor in those impact points will help ensure that the boots have what it takes to fully protect your feet.

### Conclusion

Remember that the point of all your gear is to cover your body fully, protecting you as much as possible from the elements and the consequences of any accidents. Buying gear that fits well is crucial.

you may ever find, the potential for injury is always going to be greater than when you travel by car. It's a given. Why take unnecessary chances with serious head injury? Everything you are, every memory and every skill, is housed there. Your noggin deserves the protection.

## Helmet Standards

There are a number of studies on specifications and standards governing impact absorption in motorcycle helmets, how one differs

Full-face helmet

from another, and their relevancy in protecting your head. These standards include the DOT standard and the Snell Memorial Foundation (a private testing organization) M2010 standard, as well the European ECE 22-05 standard and the British BSI 6658 Type A standard. Although I have read some truly excellent articles discussing the differences between these standards, the scope of this book does not lend itself to an in-depth discussion. I can, however, say this: getting a helmet that meets

## Consider This

The laws of physics say that the highest force is generated at the end of a lever arm. On a motorcycle, the rotational axis is where the bike's wheels contact the pavement—and at the end of that "lever arm" is your head. The rotational force generated with a sideways fall-down crash will concentrate the most force to the upper part of your body, and the snapping motion of your body hitting the ground will almost always cause your head to hit as well. This does not even begin to approach the kinds of forces generated in a frontal impact crash.

safety standards is essential for real head protection.

Helmets must carry a DOT certification in order to be legal for sale and use on the roads and highways in the United States. You will also find the Snell Foundation standard or ECE 22-05 certification on helmets that are certified to these standards. The DOT and Snell standards are the ones you are most likely to see when buying a helmet in the States. Helmets designed to these standards feature a state-of-the-art, shock-absorbing inner liner and an extensive padding system designed to dissipate shock to the head and the neck.

## Types of Helmets

Full-face helmets offer the greatest degree of protection, and virtually all helmets of this type come with a face shield and, thus, incorporate eye protection into their design. Dirt, dust, bugs, birds, rocks, and road debris are ever-present hazards when you're riding. If you're riding without eye protection, contact from any of these objects can range from irritating to seriously eye-damaging and can lead to a serious accident should you lose control of the bike because of pain or momentary loss of sight.

Face shields come in many colors and many levels of tinting, but I recommend getting a clear or, at most, a very lightly tinted face shield. There may be times when you find yourself on the road later than planned or as the sky darkens with the onset of a thunderstorm, or you may unexpectedly find yourself going through a tunnel. A clear or lightly tinted shield allows the greatest visibility in these and similar situations. On a sunny day, you can add motorcycle-specific sunglasses.

Another option is to buy two shields—one clear and one dark. You will want to carry whichever one you are not wearing in your saddlebag in case you need it. Some people prefer this option because they find getting sunglasses inside a full-face helmet difficult and the glasses themselves uncomfortable to wear. You will need to determine what works best for you.

The face shields also typically have "click stops" that allow you to open the shields fully or partially for more airflow and cooling. In the full-face helmet category are modular helmets, with face- and chin-protection sections that rotate up and out of the way, allowing you (for example) to drink water without removing your helmet.

The solid portion of a three-quarter-style helmet covers the top and back of the head as well as the ears. I would consider this the minimum protection level for a motorcyclist's head. Using this type of helmet also requires that you purchase a separate method of eye protection; most three-quarter helmets are available with attachment points for face shields.

Acceptable eye protection also includes goggles or riding glasses (tinted or untinted) that are specifically designed for motorcyclists; these must be shatterproof (usually polycarbonate). These are fairly conventional-looking (eyeglass-style) eye protection, but they incorporate a cushioned layer on the back side of the frame around the eyes to help keep out dust and dirt. I have used all of these methods and like the sunglass-style eye protection best, simply because this style allows me to remove the glasses whenever necessary (for example, to consult a map while stopped) without taking off my helmet. The three-quarter-style helmet exposes the rider to a higher level of wind noise, so when using these helmets, the rider should wear earplugs, as well (see page 66 for further discussion of earplugs).

I would also strongly suggest that you avoid half helmets that do not cover the ears, or cover

Three-quarter-style helmet

them with only cloth or leather, as well as novelty helmets that offer very little in the way of protection for your head. In addition, many of these half helmets are not DOT certified and, as such, would not be legal in a state where helmets are required.

Wearing a DOT-certified helmet while you ride will increase not only your safety but also your comfort. It will keep your head warmer in the winter, dry in the rain, and protected from direct sun in the summer. In the cold, body temperature is lost primarily through the head and the hands. Keeping these areas warm in cold- or wet-weather riding will greatly increase comfort and help prevent the danger of hypothermia. In the summer, a vented full-face helmet (almost all manufacturers incorporate open-close air vents in helmets) or an open-face helmet with a visor will help keep your head cooler and direct sun and sunburn at bay. (See Tilting at Helmet Windmills, page 66.)

## Purchasing a Helmet

Some final words on purchasing a helmet: sizes and interior dimensions are not standardized. One manufacturer's "large" could be another's "extra-large" or "medium," and head shapes differ. Buying a helmet on the Internet might cost you less (although not necessarily), but this is one purchase you should definitely make at a retail location where there are plenty of helmets available to try on.

Once again, comfort is a key factor—while a helmet should be snug around your head and remain relatively stable and in place when you move your head (and even shake it), you should not be able to pull it off once the chin strap is fastened. Realize that the discomfort of pressure points and excessively tight contact areas on your head will be magnified after a relatively short riding time. Those working in motorcycle dealerships or retail locations are usually motorcyclists themselves, and they can often assist in purchasing a helmet that is a good fit for your head. (See Make Sure Your Gear Fits, pages 62–63.)

## Earplugs

Complete ear coverage is important for another very good reason—to reduce wind noise. In addition to your helmet, you will want to use some kind of earplugs to further increase your level of ear protection. There are well-documented cases of hearing loss in motorcycle riders as a result of long-term exposure to wind noise.

There's no requirement that you have to sacrifice your hearing to participate in

There are many types of earplugs for riders.

the motorcycling lifestyle, so make sure that your ears are protected.

Contrary to what you might think, standard foam or industrial-type earplugs will not completely block external noise. Think of wearing earplugs as akin to rolling up the windows in your car. You will still hear the engine of your motorcycle, the horns of cars, the sounds of trucks and other large vehicles, and the sirens of emergency vehicles, but the earplugs will lower overall volume and block most of the higher-frequency noise, such as wind.

A variety of earplugs are available, including custom-molded ones that are sold through companies that specialize in ear protection for motorcycle riders. While some riders will find these more

# Tilting at Helmet Windmills

The single most important piece of gear in your motorcycling wardrobe is a good-quality helmet. Yet currently, there are only twenty states that mandate the use of a helmet, twenty-seven that require some helmet use, and three that have no helmet law at all. Why? Because many bikers feel the government shouldn't tell people what they should or should not wear. If you are a rider

who believes that not wearing a helmet or wearing a novelty helmet that essentially offers no protection is a way to protest government control, then you're tilting at windmills and putting yourself in jeopardy. A good-quality helmet is your best protection against serious head injury and permanent brain damage.

However, if you're the type of person who believes that proper-

fitting DOT and Snell helmets do not reduce the potential for head injury, then you may also believe that the world is flat and no astronaut ever walked on the moon. If that's the case, you may as well skip right over all of the information on helmets in this chapter. There is no amount of persuasion or discussion that will sway your opinion about the effectiveness of a helmet.

comfortable, they are, as you might guess, much more expensive than other types of earplugs.

Whichever earplugs you choose, you will find that it is less mentally taxing to ride in a quieter environment, which in turn extends your peak performance and concentration for a longer period of riding time.

## Protective Clothing

When I began riding, I wore denim jeans and a leather jacket or vest for daily riding in warm weather, a lined leather jacket for cooler months, and either military-style or hiking boots. All of that worked well enough at the time, but as I acquired more experience on the motorcycle and traveled more, I came to realize the importance of armored, made-for-motorcycling protective wear and invested in it.

Over the past decade, many advances have been made in protective clothing for the motorcyclist in terms of both comfort and level of protection, and it is a good idea to take advantage of the new technologies now available.

### Jackets and Pants

Protective clothing takes many forms and styles, from the traditional leather jackets and chaps to updated leather jackets with vented panels and jeans with Kevlar reinforcement, as well as lighter, more breathable riding suits that feature armor pads in the shoulders, elbows, back, knees, thighs, and hips. Newer types of motorcycling-specific clothing use an open-air mesh construction with protective padding that allows airflow through the suit to keep you cooler in hot weather (as long as you are moving).

In addition to the protective nature of clothing that is specific to motorcycling, there is the advantage that much of it is designed with a higher visibility factor in mind. The use of bright colors and retroreflective panels are incorporated to make the wearer easier to spot in traffic.

Here is another finding from the Hurt Report, this one on the issue of visibility:

The failure of motorists to detect and recognize motorcycles in traffic is the predominating cause of [multivehicle] motorcycle accidents. The driver of the other vehicle involved in collision with the motorcycle did not see the motorcycle before the collision, or did not see the motorcycle until too late to avoid the collision. Conspicuity of the motorcycle is a critical factor in the multiple vehicle accidents, and accident involvement is significantly reduced by the use of motorcycle headlamps (on in daylight) and the wearing of high visibility yellow, orange, or bright red jackets.

Whether you take advantage of the new technologies in motorcycle-specific gear or prefer traditional leather, wear something protective. I cringe when I see a rider who wears a full-face helmet

These are some of the latest high-tech motorcycle jackets. Mesh jackets keep you cooler than leather ones, whether you're moving or not.

with shorts, a tank top, and sandals. In these circumstances, any mishap, even a minor one, is a sure route to broken bones, road-rash burns and scars, and asphalt buried in the skin that may never be fully removed. An accident without stout clothing is much more damaging, much more dangerous, and much more painful and takes far longer for the rider to recover from than one in which the rider wears even the minimum protection of basic denim.

## Rainsuits

If you ride a motorcycle with any frequency, you will eventually get rained on, and it will happen many times over the years. One of the most uncomfortable situations you will encounter is riding while soaked by rain, especially for a long distance. Realize that even moving at moderate speeds in a light rainstorm will push water into any and every

A rainsuit will not only keep you dry but also help prevent hypothermia.

available opening in your clothing—buttons, zippers, collars, gloves, and boot tops.

Even in the summer, riding wet in the cooler temperatures that often accompany a rainstorm can not only be very uncomfortable but also can dangerously lower your body's core temperature and cause hypothermia. A good rainsuit or waterproof gear is a must.

Rainsuit collars are designed to go under a helmet, directing water outside of the water-resistant layer. And while any setup may not be 100 percent watertight, the combination of a helmet and rainsuit will go a long way toward keeping you dry. Trying to get by with less than the proper gear will mean that you're likely to be soaked in a rainstorm. No question—spend the money.

**Streetmasters Advice from *Walt Fulton***

# Don't Chill Out

It's no surprise to motorcyclists that a small drop in ambient temperature makes a big change in rider comfort; the reason for this is the windchill factor. For example, riding at 70 miles per hour in a temperature of 45 degrees Fahrenheit will feel more like 31 degrees! It's particularly important for motorcyclists to be acutely aware of the body's reaction as the ambient temperatures get colder, and not just because of the discomfort it causes.

Your body's core temperature is usually about 98.6 degrees Fahrenheit. Physiologically, a mere 1- to 2-degree drop in your core temperature will cause you to shiver and your hands to become numb as the blood vessels constrict in the fingers. Losing tactile sensation certainly can be a major problem when you are trying to coordinate use of the throttle, clutch, front brake, and

This is Yosemite's Tioga Pass Road just after its opening in the spring. Get the right cold-weather gear so you don't miss out.

## Gloves and Boots

Buying gloves and boots designed specifically for motorcycling is a smart move. Complete coverage of the hands prevents sunburn, shields them against bugs and road debris while you're riding, and protects against road rash as well as permanent skin damage in the event of an accident.

Gloves with reinforced knuckles protection

Gloves with extra padding or gel inserts are also made to isolate the hands from vibration and make holding the handlebars in one position for a long period of time more comfortable.

Motorcycling gloves are frequently manufactured for seasonal use, with light-duty and ventilated varieties for warmer climes and times of the year, and more-insulated types for cold-weather riding. Purchase gloves that are waterproof. It's a good idea to buy winter gauntlet-style gloves that have plastic covers attached in pockets at the wrist. If your motorcycle is equipped with a power outlet or you elect to have one added to your bike, consider electrically heated gloves (and other heated clothing) designed for cold-weather riding. (See Don't Chill Out below.)

Boots designed for motorcycling often extend to midcalf and have high-traction soles. Styles range from traditional lace-ups to more modern varieties with waterproof materials, water-resistant zippers, and Velcro overlaps. Most high-quality boots will have shin, ankle, and toe protection to shield the lower legs, where the bones are closer to the body's surface and thus more vulnerable to injury. They also give more support to the lower leg, ankle, and foot, which helps keep your feet in solid contact with the ground when you are supporting the bike.

Motorcycle-enthusiast magazines periodically publish articles that compare, review, and rate all types of protective gear, and a little research can go a long way in helping you make good choices. Helmets are typically rated for level of protection, ease of use (for example, regarding straps and visors), and level of sound transmission (wind noise). Protective suits, gloves, and boots are rated for comfort, ease of use, and protection level. If you cannot find issues of magazines that have reviewed these items, you should find previously published articles on the Internet.

steering. More importantly, colder body temperatures slow reaction times and impair judgment.

It's usually easy to keep your legs warm, but toes suffer the same consequences as fingers during an extended ride time and exposure to cold weather. This makes rear brake use and shifting an awkward proposition. Even a task as simple as putting a foot down at a stop can be a challenge. Without the proper gear, you should plan to stop more frequently to thaw out.

There was a time when layering was the only solution for protecting yourself as temperatures dropped, but how many layers can you wrap your hands in and still maintain the needed tactile communication with the controls? Today, you have more options to consider. For the hands, feet, and body, a variety of reasonably priced chemical warmers is available. You can also purchase battery-powered socks in the range of twenty-five dollars. The problem with these options is that they're effective for a limited amount of time. The best solution, because of convenience and assured comfort, is electric gear that runs directly off of the bike's battery. You can purchase gloves, socks, a jacket, and pants that are heated and will keep you toasty warm as temperatures plummet.

While the expense for electric gear may be greater than that for buying additional layers, the advantages more than make up for the extra costs. If it's a concern, you can add one piece at a time so you don't break the bank. Arriving at your destination with fingers, toes, and a core temperature in the comfort range and you in complete control of the bike is priceless.

# CHAPTER 5

# TAKING YOUR FIRST RIDES

>>> "Ride, Sally, ride" are not only the lyrics of a classic rhythm and blues song but also excellent advice for anyone (insert name here) who wants to improve his or her motorcycling skills. The only way you are going to become a better motorcycle rider is to get out there on your bike and ride. It's as simple—and as challenging—as that.

In his book *Five Steps to Expert*, the award-winning scholar and researcher Paul G. Schempp, who has been described as an "expert on expertise," outlines the steps necessary to go from being a novice to being an expert. The steps are: 1) beginner, 2) capable, 3) competent, 4) proficient, and 5) expert. It is a straightforward formula for becoming better at anything that you want to do.

In *Five Steps to Expert*, Paul Schempp explains that you must take each step in turn.

You cannot go directly from step 1 to step 5—from beginner to expert. As your experience, knowledge, and skills increase, you move from one step to the next, developing new characteristics that will help you perform the next step. There is no substitute for experience when it comes to developing expertise. Experience offers opportunity for learning.

Schempp also states that "[p]ersonal development is an individual endeavor, and none of us develops in the same way, at the same time, or for the same reasons." In other words, don't measure your rate of riding progress against anyone else's. Take your time, set your own pace—but do get out there and practice.

In this chapter, I offer ideas for gaining riding experience and becoming more comfortable on your motorcycle. While you clearly gain experience every time you get on the bike, using the particular opportunities and environments discussed in this chapter will allow you to more fully develop the relationship between you and your motorcycle and improve your skills before you go public. Remember that the basic riding course was only the start of your education, and riding is the best way to acquire skill.

**Streetmasters Advice from *Walt Fulton***

# Strengthening Yourself for the Ride

You'll often hear that motorcycling is 80 percent mental and 20 percent physical. In reality, both the mental and physical aspects of motorcycling must be active 100 percent of the time, and they must function well together. If you are completely out of shape, you'll find it difficult to remain mentally alert. You don't have to be a Charles Atlas to ride well, but your body does need to be reasonably fit for you to be comfortable with the rigors and physical requirements of the ride.

Riding a motorcycle without a fairing or a windshield means that you will constantly be exposed to wind. Even if you have one or both, you'll discover there are times when you will get buffeted from one side or the other by a crosswind. And no matter what you ride, you will be seated in one position for perhaps hours at a time, with your legs bent and your hands resting on the handlebar. Backrest or not, this can be a tiring experience for someone who is out of shape.

To help strengthen your body for the ride, try to squeeze in a few push-ups and sit-ups on a daily basis. Consider buying some weights and building up your arm strength. Do stretching exercises, as well—before, during (at rest stops, of course), and after the ride. As you increase your riding skills and improve your physical fitness, you will find the mental and physical aspects of riding coming together to help you perform like a well-oiled machine.

Any exercise that helps you strengthen your body, such as push-ups or lifting weights, will help you get ready to ride.

You can set up parking-lot drills like those used in the MSF riding course (*above*) to practice skills, such as cornering, without the distraction of traffic.

# Drilling in Parking Lots

The safer environment of a vacant parking lot allows you to get used to your new machine's size, weight, and capabilities and to practice the maneuvers you learned in your riding course before you operate the motorcycle in a less-forgiving street environment. Take time to practice crucial techniques, such as braking at different speeds and countersteering (see page 27), in turns. As you develop a better understanding of how everything works, you also develop muscle memory, that intuitive understanding of how the bike will respond to your inputs without your consciously thinking about them. The instinctual reflexes that come with well-developed muscle memory can keep you out of trouble when the unexpected happens.

You can restrict your drills to an hour here and there, whatever works with your schedule. Just don't try to squeeze a session in when you're short on time. You don't want to feel rushed. Some established motorcycle clubs organize group parking-lot drills for their riders and use cone setups similar to those used in the Motorcycle Safety Foundation (MSF) class; they also provide facilitators to coach and monitor the drills. Club websites that encourage these drills post information about how much area (the required parking-lot dimensions) is necessary to practice in and diagrams to set up the exercises. These drills often include controlled braking, U-turns, swerving, tight right and left turns, and figure eights. Participating in parking-lot drills is a good way to improve skills and keep them sharp.

# Riding Out in the Country

One of the beauties of motorcycle riding is that congested city streets and interstate highways are usually the antithesis of what you will find most enjoyable about being on a motorcycle: riding the open road. Many urban areas have open country roads within an hour of the city limits. If you reside anywhere near foothill mountains (the kind with sedate hills and not-too-extreme curves), you have a great training ground for getting a feel for the bike. If you don't, any open country area where traffic is at a minimum will do.

This scenario allows you to practice what you learned in the basic riding course—looking where you want the bike to go, countersteering and leaning, and entering and leaving curves along the best lines as well as accelerating out of them. Take it easy, take it slow, and learn the bike. Time spent developing good riding technique early on will pay big dividends further down the road.

When I bought my first motorcycle, I lived in a northern suburb of Atlanta, and every opportunity I had, I headed away from the city into the northern Georgia Appalachian foothills to just ride. Besides simply enjoying it, I made a point of trying to analyze what I was doing and how I was doing it so I could improve my riding technique. My personal quest was to become good at this thing. While not overriding my abilities, I did try, over the weeks and months, to slightly increase my capabilities each time I rode. The lack of traffic in rural areas allowed

**Streetmasters Advice from *Walt Fulton***

## Riding Off Road

Consider taking a course on dirt-bike or dual-sport riding to improve your street-riding techniques.

If you want to be a better street-bike rider, you should spend some time learning to ride off-road. There are several good reasons for doing so.

Attempting to expand your horizons and practice new techniques in a mix of traffic or on unfamiliar roads can lead to costly mistakes. In the dirt, there are no *cages* (cars/trucks) competing for your real estate. Are you comfortable riding in the rain? Dirt riding offers you an excellent opportunity to acquire the finesse necessary to ride in low-traction street conditions, such as wet pavement, without the consequences of taking a spill in traffic. Do you have trouble making U-turns? This is one of the most basic techniques for an off-roader. Figure eights, U-turns, off-camber turns (turns banked higher on the inside than on the outside) are all dirt techniques that will transfer directly over to the street rider. And how well can you use the front brake? Are you certain you can get the most out of it? Again, less-than-ideal traction conditions teach you the finesse required in using the front brake to its maximum stopping capability.

Dirt-bike/off-road schools exist nationwide, and the MSF offers dirt-bike training courses as well. In addition, you will find off-road schools that are specific to larger displacement adventure bikes, motocross schools, and off-road touring companies—the choices are many.

Practicing new techniques in a friendly environment is a great way to learn and refine your riding skills. Improving your confidence in the dirt will transfer to your street riding, and make you a better rider all around.

Riding the foothills outside the city, during low-traffic periods, offers good opportunities to practice your skills out on the road—and in pleasant surroundings.

me to concentrate more on the motorcycle and what I was doing on it and the time and space to recover from mistakes when I made them.

*Warning*: Vigilance is always necessary, whether traffic is sparse or not. Even on a sunny Tuesday afternoon on a seemingly deserted mountain highway, there is always the chance that someone is coming the other way around that curve, close to or sometimes over the center line. This has happened to me on several occasions. Although I remained prepared, avoiding the danger usually required some immediate readjustment in my line through the curve. Do not ride faster than the time you need to react properly to other people's mistakes or to your own, and always be prepared for the unexpected.

## Consider This

You may not be twenty-five any longer, but that doesn't mean you've lost all of your competitive spirit. Competition doesn't have to be about racing down a drag strip. Instead, it can be about challenging yourself to be a better rider by increasing your skill level on the bike, whether that means mastering riding techniques in general or a specific make, model, and size of motorcycle.

# Taking Advanced Rider Courses

Down the road, when you've gathered some experience on the motorcycle, consider taking an advanced riding course. Many organizations and motorcycle manufacturers conduct advanced courses designed to help you improve your riding techniques. The MSF offers the Experienced RiderCourse (ERC), a five-and-a-half-hour class covering topics such as advanced street-riding strategies, traction management, and advanced cornering, braking, and swerving techniques. Being certified in this course could help lower your insurance rates (depending on the state where you live), but the prime motivator here should be the opportunity to develop better riding technique and improve your skills. Notable among advanced courses is the Stayin' Safe Advanced Rider Training course. Team Oregon and Idaho STAR also offer intermediate and advanced riding training courses and precision skills.

Other organizations, such as safety/skills adviser (see sidebars) and instructor Walt Fulton's Streetmasters Motorcycling Workshops and Total Control Advanced Riding Clinic, offer workshops on precision cornering skills. Some advanced-training classes are conducted on roads and highways rather than on closed courses. A student uses a one-way radio receiver inside his or her helmet while an instructor rides behind, coaching in real time. The coach suggests ways for a student to improve riding technique regarding the proper lines through curves, lane position, awareness of surroundings, and other maneuvers. Most organizations that sponsor classes have websites where you can learn more about their programs and the many types of classes offered.

At Streetmasters, a student takes a corner low and tight on one of the largest bikes, the Gold Wing. Advanced courses improve essential skills.

This is an experienced two-up riding pair, with enough time on their Gold Wing together to take a trip through the mountains on twisty roads.

# Learning Two-Up and Group Riding

Soloing on the open road is not the only way to go. You can also ride with a passenger (two-up) and with a group. Each type of riding requires a specific set of skills. I recommend not trying either type until you have been riding the bike long enough for your instincts and reactions to become more intuitive. Only you know when you are ready. I did not begin carrying a passenger until I had been solo riding regularly for more than a year. I rode with a group before I carried a passenger.

## Riding Two-Up

As you can probably imagine, having a passenger on the bike will change the feel and the performance of your bike in every aspect, including acceleration, braking, and cornering. You need to learn what to expect when you go from riding solo to riding two-up and how to handle the differences. In addition, your passenger will have to know and obey the riding rules that you learned in your basic riding course as well as understand what to do and what not to do while riding with you.

Consider taking an advanced riding course that allows you to take the class with a passenger. Many advanced training classes offer this option, and this would certainly be a great opportunity not only to take an advanced training class but also to get coaching and instruction while riding with a partner. Both of you would learn the proper techniques for two-up riding, and your partner would gain a fuller understanding of and appreciation for the maneuvering techniques you have to utilize and the capabilities of the motorcycle before you take to the road.

Whether you take a formal course with a passenger or not, I recommend that you read up on the techniques used in two-up riding in books, in magazines, and online. In his book *Proficient Motorcycling*, David Hough has an excellent section on the subject titled "The Second Rider." Hough discusses, among other subjects, how to brief your passenger about safety issues (what gear to wear, how to mount the bike), how to handle stops (leave more room for braking, brake harder), what to do when accelerating (prepare the passenger, don't be too aggressive), how to corner (tell the passenger to lean with you, follow a larger radius), and how to ride downhill (brake sooner) and uphill (shift your weight forward). You can also find information on riding two-up in magazines such as *Motorcycle Consumer News* and on motorcycling websites such as Motorcyclecruiser.com. Check the local newsstand for other bike magazines and do an Internet search for other online bike magazines, articles, opinions, and forums on this subject.

So before your passenger climbs aboard, learn as much as you can about two-up riding and share the information with him or her. Begin with an advanced riding course (if possible), move on to parking lots, and then take your passenger for a ride on open country roads away from traffic. Periodically check to make sure your passenger is as comfortable in his or her seat as you are in yours. If not, your passenger will not have a fun time riding—and neither will you. The time to work out all the details is before your first daylong two-up ride. (See Passenger as Co-rider, on page 80, for further discussion.)

## Group Riding

As you will come to know as you gather riding experience, motorcyclists see themselves as something of a fraternity. Most riders will wave to each other as they pass and are quick to become involved in conversations about roads, bikes, modifications, riding gear, and all other things motorcycling. These kinds of associations often lead to your riding with a regular group of friends or an established riding club.

Clubs may be based on model of bike (such as the Honda Gold Wing Road Riders Association), on type of motorcycle (cruiser style or sportbike motorcycles are common), or on gender (there are many women's motorcycle clubs). Riding with a well-established, rules-oriented riding club is a good way to ease back into riding, and when club members become friends, it is a great way to travel on a bike as well.

With a group, there is always a support crew of experienced riders available to answer questions,

>> A Rider's Tale
# Cathy's Story, Part 2: Keep Learning

After I passed the MSF course and got my license [see chapter 1 for Cathy's Story, Part 1], I wanted a bike that was smaller and lighter than my old 500, a bike that was easier to ride at this point in my riding career. I spent a lot of time around town and in the mountains on that bike.

Cathy on her Gold Wing, still learning and still riding

Initially, I found that my speed and skills in the mountains were still on the poor side, but as I gained more confidence, riding the motorcycle grew easier. In 2004, I bought a used 2002 Yamaha V-Star 1100 with only 315 miles on it. After I started riding the V-Star, I joined a women's riding club. I hadn't ridden in a large group before, so I observed a lot and was relieved to find that all of the group's members were very supportive of me.

The 2006 American Motorcycling Association's "Women and Motorcycling Conference" in Athens, Georgia, was simply an excuse for me and two other ladies to explore what it was like to take a long-distance ride. We planned carefully, discussing every aspect of our trip, and then safely made

A group of riders on Georgia 52, west of Dahlonega, ride in staggered formation. Make sure you know group-riding rules before you ride with a group.

our way from California to Georgia in four-and-a-half days. None of us had gone on such a long trip before.

What I learned from this first cross-country trip was that my riding skills were still somewhat weak, so I retook the MSF class. Then at an event, I met motorcycling instructor Nancy Foote, and she told me about her Streetmasters Precision Cornering Workshop. I realized that I owed it to myself to become the best rider I could and made the commitment. A year later, my daughter-in-law and I took the class, which opened my eyes to options in riding corners in the mountains. Many people commented that my riding became far better after that class! I have retaken the class after getting another motorcycle and have also taken the ERC class. In addition, I have read a variety of books about motorcycles and riding, educating myself on every aspect of riding.

assist in the event of mechanical problems, and help you learn the ropes. Usually, when you join a club, there will be some required reading on how the group rides (which covers subjects such as staggered riding formation, distances between bikes, and standard hand signals). Clubs frequently have chapters in other areas of the country, which makes finding riding companions outside your home turf easier. Although I typically take solo touring vacations now, I very much enjoyed riding with a club for the first several years after I began riding again.

*A caveat about group riding*: Not everyone knows how to lead or be a part of a group ride. When a group gets together to ride, all riders must obey the rules. The person leading the group should be experienced and show common sense; a group leader especially should know what *not* to do when leading a group of bikes. One unexpected hard-braking stop by the leader of a group and you will learn very quickly what I mean. Ride farther back and with heightened awareness of the group dynamic until you see how well the group is organized and get a feeling for the riding skill and competence level of the leaders. (There are often several leaders in different positions within the group.) If you find yourself riding with a group that is not organized and not obeying the rules for group riding, make your excuses and find your own way. One more critical piece of advice: if you find that the group's pace is faster than you can comfortably maintain, exit the group at the next stop and ride your own speed.

As with two-up riding, it's a good idea to read about the dynamics and techniques of riding with a group before you decide to join one. You will find discussions about group riding in motorcycling magazines and on websites, as well as in books.

# Commuting on the Bike

Commuting in traffic is one of the more demanding situations you can be in on a motorcycle. The levels of automobile and truck traffic are much higher during rush hour than at other times, which means that drivers are often more harried and impatient to get to work or home. Motorcycles are also less visible in the high-traffic environment. This is always a bad combination. We all know that rush-hour drivers are more likely to try to get through that yellow light and make a left turn in front of traffic—one of the most common causes of motorcycle accidents.

Then there's the fact that in the stop-and-go traffic of rush hour, motorcycling is more physically demanding and a lot less enjoyable. Your clutch

**Streetmasters Advice from *Walt Fulton***

## Passenger as Co-rider

A passenger should not be just a lump on the back of the seat. He or she is now a dynamic part of a team! Passengers have a responsibility to themselves and to a bike's operator. It's much better to take a ride and work in unison with the operator than to counteract, unknowingly, the operator's control inputs.

On a meandering road, for example, the passenger should not counterbalance (lean the wrong way) while the operator is cornering or, just as the operator is coming to a stop, get an acute case of "ants in the pants." Both of these actions require the operator to work much harder than necessary.

Even though the passenger doesn't operate the motorcycle, he or she still needs to have a working knowledge of how a bike is ridden. This is why we like to refer to the passenger as a *co-rider*. The co-rider must use many of the same riding skills that the operator does. Every movement from the co-rider is transferred through the chassis to the handlebars, where the operator must react to keep the bike on its desired path of travel. Most motorcyclists will agree that the best co-rider is one who seems like he or she is not there because that co-rider moves

This passenger knows to lean with the operator as they corner.

in conjunction with the operator.

Some passengers choose to take a beginner riding class even when they have no desire to take control of the handlebars. The class gives them a working knowledge of such subjects as how passenger movement affects the bike, how a motorcycle leans in a corner, and how important balance is. Whether your passenger takes a formal class or not, both of you should know how to ride!

Motorcycle commuting saves gas, but unless you live in California, where bikes *lane share* (ride between adjacent lanes of cars), rush hour's stop-and-go can be tiring.

hand gets a real workout, and weather conditions (especially the heat of a summer afternoon) can make being stopped in traffic very uncomfortable. Stop-and-go traffic is not great for the bike, either. Many motorcycle engines are air cooled—that is, they rely on airflow around the engine to cool it. Although many manufacturers now use some other kind of cooling system on their bikes, be that air/oil cooling or traditional radiators with liquid coolant, airflow is still a large part of maintaining optimum operating temperature. So being in conditions with low airflow (such as stop-and-go traffic) may cause an engine to run hot, placing more stress on the mechanicals.

You may be one of the lucky riders who live in a small town with low traffic levels or work at a location that is removed from traffic so that a commute on the motorcycle would be a great way to start and end a workday. For those who toil in metropolitan areas, commuting by motorcycle could be a less enjoyable option. That is certainly not to say that you should avoid acquiring experience in high-traffic

environments. This is a part of learning to ride in all situations, and one that you will undoubtedly have to deal with many times. I recommend, however, that new and returning riders avoid these situations at the beginning of the learning curve.

Once you have gotten a decent amount of riding experience and, hence, a more intuitive comfort-level operating the bike, you might consider plunging into the craziness of rush hour. Or you may prefer not to put your bike and your body through the added stress. You may conclude that in this situation, it's wiser to take the car.

Even after riding for over a decade, and when I was still working five days a week from nine to five, I would only occasionally take the bike to work. Not because I was intimidated by the high-traffic environment, but because of the riding conditions. I just didn't like it much. After work on a great summer evening (when the sun was still up past 8 p.m.), I would take the bike out and head for unpopulated rural areas, where I enjoyed the ride a lot more.

# CHAPTER 6

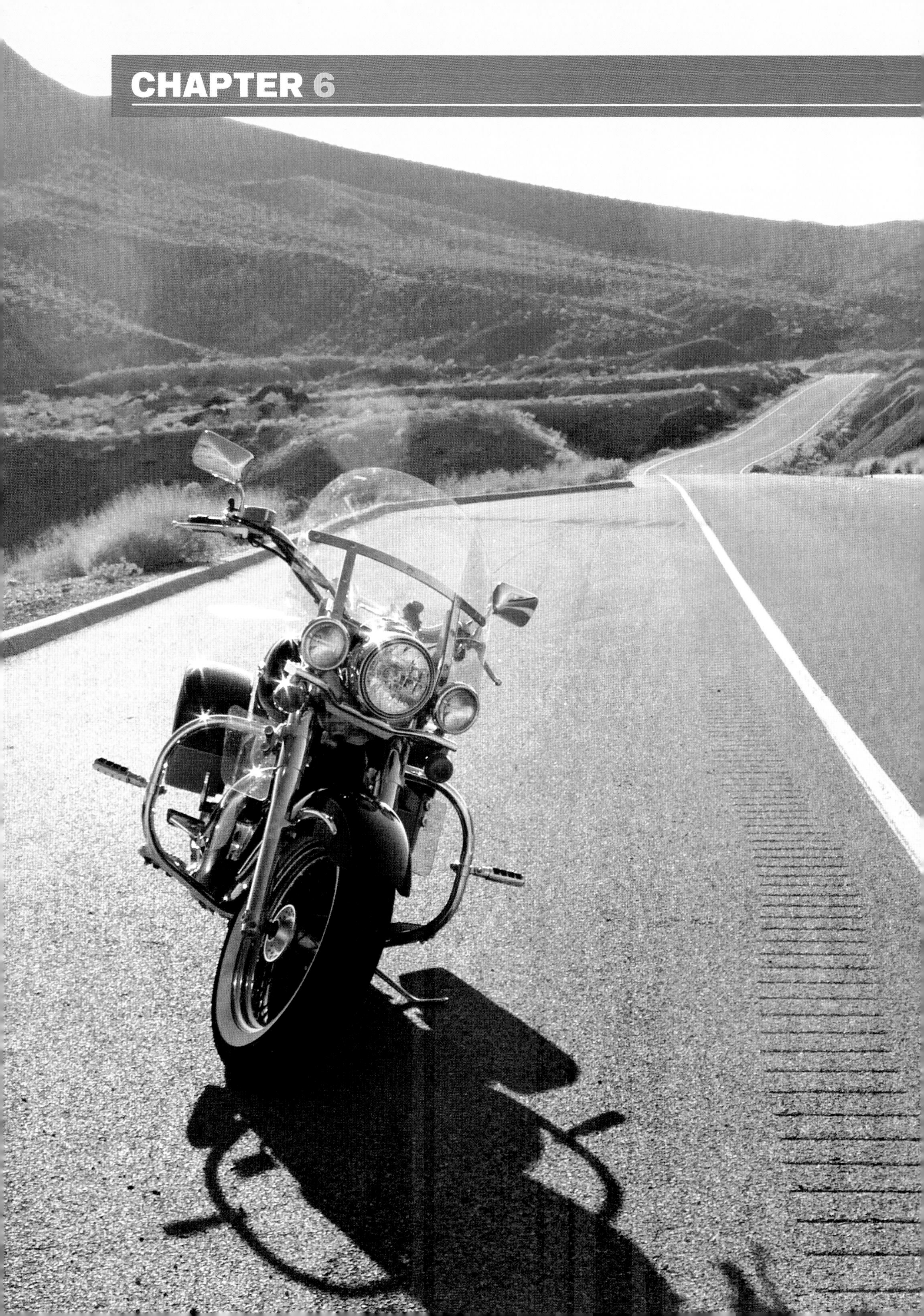

# VENTURING OUT ON YOUR FIRST TOURS

>> So now you've acquired some experience, and you're ready to try traveling longer distances on the motorcycle. Start logically, and think "weekend excursion" rather than "weeklong tour." Do you have any friends or relatives within a four- or five-hour drive that are due a visit? Favorite vacation spots within that distance? These are the kinds of close-by adventures that work well as beginning touring experiences.

At the time I began riding again, I had family in western North Carolina, about 240 miles away from where I lived, in Atlanta. The roads leading there included scenic routes, such as the Blue Ridge Parkway, as well as many scarcely traveled two-lane country highways. I found riding to see family the perfect first-time motorcycle travel experience.

# The Preparations: What to Bring, What to Leave

As I soon learned, traveling by motorcycle proved to be much more fun than traveling by automobile. When you travel by motorcycle, the riding itself frequently becomes much of the focus of your vacation. When I first started going out on short

At the very least, you'll want to have sturdy leather saddlebags for carrying basic items; ones with locks would be even better.

tours, I went on a number of weekend rides over a period of several months and learned that I could take a bike anywhere that I could take an automobile, as long as I was properly prepared to travel on a motorcycle.

The key to being properly prepared for motorcycle travel is knowing what you should bring and what you should not bring with you. Bear in mind that storage space will be at a premium. At least you won't have to worry about space for your riding gear because you will be wearing it. Everything else, however, needs to fit into whatever

saddlebags and extra storage containers that you may have.

There are some items that you will want to have in a saddlebag almost anytime that you travel, whether you are going for an afternoon ride or going on a weeklong tour. These will, of course, vary somewhat for everyone.

The items I usually carry include:

- A cell phone
- A rainsuit
- A lightweight bike cover (many fold into small bags)
- A motorcycle-specific cable and lock system
- Maps of destination and route options (I keep state maps in a saddlebag and a map of the route in a clear-cover magnetic tank bag so I can consult it as necessary.)
- Basic safety items, such as a flashlight, a "help-needed" sign, a small tool kit, and supplies for minor repairs or adjustments
- A tire repair kit and a can of tire sealant, in case I get a flat on a deserted road (See page 55 for cautions on using tire sealant.)

Other items that I bring along are a camera and a GPS. As a large percentage of the storage space is often taken up by the items listed above, packing room for clothing is usually not abundant. Packing clothing requires a spartan mind-set, but that usually works out because you're not likely to need evening wear. After a day on the bike, you'll probably want R and R, rather than a night out on the town. A few pairs of your most comfortable jeans, some comfortable shirts, and a comfy second pair of shoes (along with required personal items) will suffice. If the weather warrants it, bring a bathing suit for a jump in the pool, lake, or ocean (on a hot day), or bring polyester or silk undergarments to wear under the riding suit should a sudden cold snap occur. If a riding vacation does coincide with an event requiring upscale dress, consider shipping dress clothes ahead to a relative or possibly to your hotel to save the packing space.

## The Excursions: How to Go, Where to Stay

For your first few excursions, minimize the likelihood of a less-than-enjoyable experience. Pick a dry, high-pressure-weather weekend with comfortable temperatures at whatever time of the year is best in your area of the country to lessen the possibility that you'll run into bad weather. With that rainsuit stowed in your saddlebag, you will be prepared for rain, but there's no reason to ride through it if you can avoid it. Choose a location you can travel to in less than eight hours with stops factored in. Don't be in a rush to get to your destination. As I said earlier, much of the fun of traveling by motorcycle lies in the journey itself.

### How to Go

There are few things more boring than riding a motorcycle for hours on a typical interstate highway. Because most cars and virtually all large trucks take the interstates, those routes are often crowded and sometimes crazy, with drivers focused on getting to their destinations as fast as possible. You will come to appreciate riding "the road less traveled," with little or sometimes no traffic, which usually

**Streetmasters Advice from *Walt Fulton***

## Get the Big Picture

If you were asked what the most important technique in motorcycling is, how would you answer? There certainly are a number of potential answers to this question: head and eyes up; look through the corner; be smooth with the throttle, clutch, and brakes; slow before a corner. The list goes on.

My answer: get the big picture. The big picture is akin to situational awareness, and it's a two-step concept that assists you in determining what your next move will be.

The first step in getting the big picture requires you to aggressively search for clues about the roadway surface, traffic flow, signal lights, where the road goes, and any other important aspect that could affect your riding at the moment. The second step requires you to accurately interpret all the information you have just gathered. At this point, you need to compute trajectories, consider the what-if scenarios, and call on previously stored data to interpolate the speed, lean angle, corner geometry, and braking points, as well as any other factors that are important for a location or a scenario seconds into the future.

Without getting the big picture, how will you know when to roll on the throttle, when to use the clutch and shift and the brakes to slow, and how much to slow before a corner? All of these decisions and control inputs are dependent on your getting the big picture.

This is a dynamic situation, that is, one that is ever changing. You must always be thinking into the future.

*The changing light at sunset requires a greater degree of situational awareness when you're interpreting the big picture.*

Running from Georgia to Florida, US Route 41 is the scenic alternative to Interstate 75. Take the scenic route whenever possible.

translates into a more relaxed and safer ride. I highly recommend taking the scenic backcountry routes; you'll find the ride more interesting and the travel unhurried, unharried, and more pleasurable.

You will also be surprised by all the off-the-beaten-track roads and areas out there to explore. Even when you have visited your chosen destination many times by car (via the interstates), you will find that traveling on smaller highways or backcountry roads to get there will open your eyes to places and sights you've missed, including quaint towns you never knew existed. Many small towns on rural routes and highways have remained very much the same for decades, giving you a sense that you're riding through an earlier, less frenetic time.

Of course, traveling the scenic routes and rural highways means that, most often, you will not be able to maintain the mile-a-minute average speed of the interstate—so getting to a destination will take longer. The exception here is that rural roads occasionally offer more direct routes than do the interstates, which compensates for the slower travel time.

Whatever your choice of route, plan for the mode of transportation. If possible, avoid making reservations and tying yourself to a tight schedule. When traveling on the bike, you will sometimes decide to change your itinerary or the route to your destination. You might decide to take a detour to explore a recommended or more interesting route or to avoid bad weather, make an unplanned stop at a location along the way, or simply underestimate or overestimate the time it takes to get to a destination.

Avoid holiday weekends or the most traveled vacation times so that traffic is lighter and hotel rooms are more likely to be available on a walk-in basis. By doing so, you can change plans on the fly more easily and won't have to pay for hotel reservations you can't keep. If you do find yourself traveling over the holidays, however, taking a rural highway may be not only the more scenic and relaxing option but also the timelier one for reaching your holiday destination. That's been the case for me a number of times.

Having lived in the Atlanta area, I know that locations in Florida are popular vacation destinations for those who live in Georgia's capital. The primary route from Atlanta to Florida is Interstate 75. On heavily traveled holiday weekends, such as Memorial Day, Labor Day, and Thanksgiving, traffic going south at the beginning of the weekend and north into Atlanta at the end of the weekend can back up for hours and miles. US Route 41, a two-lane rural highway that parallels I-75 virtually all the way into Florida, is mostly ignored by those wanting to get there and back as quickly as possible. The road has a speed limit of 55 miles per hour over most of its length, as well as long sections of unpopulated area that support speeds that rival those of the interstate. When I traveled this road on holiday weekends and rode beneath an interstate overpass, I often saw high traffic volumes and high-pressure driving, moving at approximately the same pace that I was maintaining on the rural road. On this state highway, only widely dispersed small towns slow progress, but these towns are good places for breaks and make the ride that much more interesting.

Old storefronts, such as these in Waynesville, Georgia, give you a feeling of stepping back in time. Small towns are another reason to take the back roads.

## Where to Stay

If you're planning on staying in hotels along the way, try to find full-service hotels that have at least a restaurant on the premises, and depending on your wants and needs, a lounge, a coin-operated laundry facility, and maybe even a convenience store. Hotels of this type are often found in or near larger towns and cities and are generally more convenient for motorcycle travel. Staying at full-service hotels will keep you from having to get back on the bike to go out for dinner or entertainment and allow you to stock up on supplies (bottled water, snacks). These hotels may not offer the best cuisine or entertainment in town (though sometimes they do!). After riding all day, however, no matter how enjoyable the travel, you're more likely to want to unwind, have dinner and maybe a beverage of choice, and call it a day. With a full-service hotel, there's even room service and a movie to watch.

**Streetmasters Advice from *Walt Fulton***

# Riding over the Edge

There's no question that summertime is the peak season for motorcycling. It's a wonderful time to travel the highways and byways of this diverse country. However, for most areas not in the southwestern part of mainland United States or in Hawaii, chances are quite high that it is also the peak season for road construction. Generally speaking, construction zones have a great potential for ruining an outing for motorcyclists. Aside from chip sealing, grooved asphalt, sand, gravel, and debris associated with road construction, motorcyclists must be ever vigilant for exposed manhole covers, or worse yet, the dreaded uneven edge break, where the pavement of two adjacent lanes come together and one lane is higher than the other.

As with other roadway issues, handling an edge break on a bike is not hard to do if you learn the

Workers often leave uneven edges, metal plates, and trenches on streets that are undergoing repair. Knowing how to handle edges and other obstacles is crucial for a rider's safety.

proper technique beforehand and perform it correctly. The technique is simple: When changing lanes over an edge break, you want the front tire to climb up and over the break. Like riding over railroad tracks, you must approach an edge, going up or down, at a greater angle (as opposed to riding nearly parallel to it) by making a definite steering input to turn into the break as you negotiate it. Relaxing shoulders and arms while firmly holding on to the bars as the front and rear wheels ride over the edge ensures a smooth transition with no extraneous steering input.

Problems develop when a rider tries to negotiate an edge break at too shallow an angle. Then the front tire may get trapped by the edge and turn under. This can lead to bike instability; tense up and you have created the potential for an even bigger problem.

Clearly loaded up for long-distance travel, these classic motorcycles sport several essential pieces of traveling equipment, including windshields.

# The Bike Options

There are certain convenience items that can be added to a bike to make traveling, and riding in general, a bit more comfortable. They include a windshield, auxiliary storage, a GPS, auxiliary lighting, a throttle lock, a power outlet, and possibly some type of communications or entertainment system.

### A Windshield

I consider a windshield a must for traveling. Full-size touring motorcycles have them, and many smaller touring cruisers are often sold with them as well, so you may already have a windshield on your motorcycle. If you bought a bike without one and traveling is on the agenda, you'll want to add it. A windshield should be tall enough to create an envelope behind it that directs the wind over your head and off of your chest but low enough for you to see over by several inches. As mentioned on page 72, a windshield goes a long way toward minimizing fatigue from having the wind push on your body all day long; it also lowers wind noise and helps divert rain, birds, and bugs around you. You should also consider *lowers*, which are small wind deflectors that mount on the front fork tubes and help keep wind from flowing under the windshield and into your torso.

Some riders prefer a taller windshield, one they look through rather than over. During rain and night riding, however, I am not in favor of looking through anything that might restrict vision and detail. Some bikes designed for traveling (usually higher-end, more expensive motorcycles) have electrically adjustable windshields that can be set at different heights (by a control on the handlebar). This is an exceptional travel amenity to have but is available on relatively few motorcycles.

### Auxiliary Lighting and Reflectors

As previously discussed, among the best safety features you can add to a bike are those that increase your visibility. Additional lighting obviously falls into this category. Touring motorcycles and touring cruisers frequently have a stock triple-light arrangement on the front of the bike. Two smaller auxiliary lights are on either side of the headlight and operate with the headlight or independently, by means of a secondary switch. Aftermarket companies make auxiliary light systems for various types of motorcycles. The latest 10W LED auxiliary lights can be used even on bikes with low-power alternators. These lights are good to have not only because they make riders more visible in traffic but also because they offer extra light for riders to see the road ahead if they are traveling at night.

Wearing riding clothing with reflective patches or attaching retroreflective tape to your helmet or your jacket and pants are also very good ways to increase visibility for nighttime riding.

A triple light bar makes a bike more visible; a rider can also see farther at night.

## ❯❯❯ A Rider's Tale
# Phyllis's Story: Venturing out on a Pretty Harley

My passion for motorcycling really began as a teenager, after my dad and my brother taught me to ride on their dirt bikes. But college, starting my career, and life in general stopped me from listening to my inner voice, which told me motorcycling was something I would truly enjoy.

However, in 2001, my perspective on life changed. After a year of dealing with and recovering from the effects of Lyme disease, turning forty, and living in New York City through the terrorist attacks of 9/11, I realized that life really is short and we must enjoy our time on earth.

A 1996 Yamaha Virago was my learning bike. Eventually, I worked my way up to my dream motorcycle. Today, I am the proud owner of a 2008 Harley-Davidson Heritage Softail in pink and black. My first road trip on the bike was in May 2008, when I accompanied some friends to Washington, DC, to attend the Rolling Thunder Rally. After several people at the rally had stopped by to comment on what a "pretty bike" I had, one of my friends turned to me and said: "I've been riding thirty-five f___ing years, and I never heard a Harley being referred to as pretty!" At that moment, I realized that I had made a very wise investment.

Through motorcycling, my life has changed for the better in so many ways. I have great friends, fun times, and memorable rides. In the first three years of riding my Harley, I put more than 11,000 miles on the bike. I have thousands of stories, and I am always looking for new adventures in the wind. I can't imagine my life without my bike or without being a member of the

## Throttle Lock

Many of the larger touring motorcycles, including touring cruisers, now have cruise control as a standard feature or an option, but this generally applies only to a company's top-of-the-line products. A mechanical cruise control of sorts, called a throttle lock, is a holding mechanism for the throttle, and an addition to the bike that can go a long way toward relieving hand fatigue when you're traveling on an extensive, straight, open road. Although it holds the throttle firmly, the throttle lock still allows adjustment of the control to vary steady speed. Of course, it should be used only where common sense dictates—outside town and on uncrowded roads—and never when riding in the rain—but it can really add to long-distance riding comfort.

The throttle lock is in the open position, and the throttle functions normally.

The lock is snapped down, holding the throttle in position.

Phyllis Lamattina with her pink and black Harley-Davidson Heritage Softail

## Auxiliary Storage

Auxiliary storage, while not a necessity, is certainly a convenience. In addition to saddlebags or lockable hard bags, you can attach a hard-case travel trunk to the bike behind the passenger seat to provide more packing space for longer tours, which is especially useful for two-up riding. These, however, are usually expensive items. A more cost-effective option would be a travel bag (soft luggage made for motorcycling), which is a waterproof or water-resistant bag that straps to the bike behind the rider. In some cases, these bags are designed to be attached on the passenger seat, so if you use one, you won't be able to carry a passenger. If you use one of these travel bags and also want to a carry passenger, you will need to add a travel rack that attaches over the rear fender to support the bag. Yes, it can get a little complicated to allow for all contingencies when traveling by motorcycle.

motorcycling community. I have started my own production company in New York City, as well, after receiving my master's degree in media and film. I am concentrating my company's productions on the motorcycle community, as there are many stories out there that need telling.

In retrospect, I am happy that I waited until my forties to become a full-fledged "biker chick," as the accomplishment is that much sweeter.

## Power Outlet

Touring bikes usually offer some kind of auxiliary power outlet. Available for any bike is a power outlet that connects to the electrical system. Outlets are useful for powering a GPS or heated gloves (wonderful in colder weather) or for charging a cell phone.

## GPS Unit

These units are good for finding a gas station or a restaurant when needed or a hotel address at the end of a long riding day. One of the best reasons to have one is that a GPS can lead you back to familiar territory if you get lost—which is very reassuring in the mountains, in a wilderness area, or on a lonely stretch of unfamiliar road. There are times, though, when you're better off relying on your map and some common sense.

On a weeklong tour of the Blue Ridge Parkway in 2009, I used a GPS on a motorcycle tour for the first time. I attached the unit, actually designed for car use, to the handlebar using an aftermarket mounting kit, which made the GPS easily available during the ride. This particular unit only had three hours of battery life, and my bike did not have a power outlet at the time, so I had to recharge the unit

I got smart and installed a power outlet on my bike.

using a wall outlet adapter when I stopped at a hotel for the night. Manufacturers of newer GPS units specific to motorcycling claim a battery life of up to twenty hours. Even so, if you want to use a GPS on a daily basis on your bike, consider purchasing a motorcycle-specific unit and adding a power outlet to the bike for convenience.

On my 2009 trip, the GPS certainly simplified finding several locations during the week—the most important, a hotel in Banner Elk, North Carolina, when, after a very long day on the motorcycle and with evening rapidly approaching, I wanted to find a room as quickly as possible. The unit was also very efficient in its directions from the Blue Ridge Parkway to a restaurant outside of Roanoke, Virginia, where my family was meeting for dinner. But the GPS wasn't always as reliable in picking the best route out on the road.

My first miscue with the unit occurred when I was traveling from the Blue Ridge Parkway to Smith Mountain Lake in Virginia. Operator inexperience this time—I programmed the unit for "shortest distance" instead of "fastest route." The shortest distance was straight through a series of increasingly isolated mountain roads whose surfaces got rougher and less maintained as I proceeded; eventually I decided to backtrack to take a more traveled route. The detour added an hour to an already long riding day.

I consider a GPS essential for all motorcycles. It's gotten me out of some tough spots.

Not that the "fastest route" is always the best one, either. During the week, I used the GPS's fastest-route option to get to a family barbecue at a mountain hotel. As I rode south on the Blue Ridge Parkway, the unit directed me to a small and unmarked gravel road at a right angle to the parkway. I passed this road at first because it looked like a hiking trail. When the unit indicated that I should make a U-turn, I went back and cautiously started down the gravel road. Within 100 yards, the road deteriorated into a ruddy, muddy dirt trail with puddles and soft mud 6 inches deep in some places. I had to struggle with Y turns, Z turns, and several other turns covering letters of the alphabet to get the bike turned around.

Later, I consulted a map, which showed the option of taking US Route 221 and paved roads almost all the way to the mountain hotel location, with a decently maintained gravel road for the last mile to the hotel, so I am not certain why the GPS selected the route that included the unimproved dirt road. In all fairness, the unit I used was already several years old in 2009, so many of the miscues I experienced probably had to do with both the unit's age and my inexperience with GPS options.

As GPS technology advances, algorithms for these units continue to become more sophisticated. Even so, a rider needs to know when a GPS unit's choice of route should be questioned and checked against a map. There is no doubt, however, that the GPS can be a useful safety tool, especially when you need to find food, lodging, or fuel in a hurry. I use a GPS on every tour now, but I also keep a map handy.

## Sounds, Man

For a beginning or returning rider, it's dangerous to use any kind of auxiliary sound system; the rider needs to stay focused and minimize distraction. It's also not a good idea for any rider to listen to music when in rush-hour traffic or any other urban-riding situation.

That being said, as an experienced rider, I find that having my favorite tunes playing while riding a great stretch of road is like having a soundtrack to my own motion picture. Generally, only the larger touring bikes have integrated sound systems, but there are many simpler options for listening to music while riding. For example, I use an MP3 player and earbud-style headphones (some types double as earplugs) inside the helmet. In addition, some manufacturers sell motorcycle-specific sound systems that incorporate intercoms (for rider-to-passenger and bike-to-bike communications) along with audio players and satellite radio receivers. These systems typically use headphones installed inside the helmet as well. You might want to avoid a setup that uses standard on-air (AM and FM) radio, as AM reception can be affected by an engine's electromagnetic force (EMF), which generates noise in AM radio frequencies. (Factory-installed motorcycle sound systems, however, will not have this problem.) FM reception can be difficult to receive outside urban areas.

Having sound systems to enhance your riding experience and communications systems that keep you informed and increase your awareness may be very worthwhile. The higher-end motorcycle communications systems feature top-of-the-line rider-to-passenger or bike-to-bike intercom systems with Bluetooth technology and an integrated music source. Simpler systems may include nothing more complicated than an MP3 player with a radio to play music and give you weather, traffic, and other important information. The use and operation of any type of audio or informational system (including those designed for and incorporated into motorcycles as standard equipment) should be easy and direct so your attention is always focused where it should be: on your riding and your surroundings.

# CHAPTER 7

# TRAVELING LONG DISTANCES

» How far can you go, really? Well, you can go as far as you have the time, ambition, stamina—and finances—to go. Some people have no problem putting in long days in the saddle; others prefer a shorter day with more leisure time. Above all, motorcycling should be about doing what is most enjoyable for the rider.

Of course, the amount of riding you like to do may also change over time. In many cases, the enjoyment of traveling by motorcycle increases as overall experience increases. Once riders have spent more time on their bikes, increased their skill levels, and gained more confidence in their abilities, many of them are ready to travel farther afield. The only limiting factor may be the amount of leisure time available.

If you live in the United States, the amount of time you have for a riding vacation may be limited. Most folks here get only two or three weeks of vacation a year (unless you're self-employed or in a profession such as teaching, where you may have summers off). So if you can't take scenic routes and backcountry roads and travel the entire way on your bike because of time limits, then consider the travel options that follow to help you get to your destination quickly to make the most of a riding adventure.

I moved cross-country in 2010, my bike securely transported in this trailer. I took the bike out for day trips, while my brother drove the car, pulling the trailer.

## » A Rider's Tale
# Eric's Story: Distance versus Posterior Comfort

I have been an avid bicyclist for many years, but the commitment to raise a family kept me from having that "Honey, I would like to ride a motorcycle" conversation with my wife. In my fiftieth year, coming off a great cycling season, I took a job about 25 miles from my house. This was either 25 miles of Interstate 270 in Maryland or 25 miles of beautiful rolling farmland the back way. Well, 50 miles round-trip was a bit far for me on my bicycle, and 2 gallons a day, five days a week, in the car was too costly. So I went through the "maybe I should get a scooter" exercise. I soon realized that a scooter wouldn't hack the trip either (at least not a small one) and decided I need to have the talk with my wife.

My wife initially accused me of taking the job 25 miles away as a plot to gain her reluctant approval. But weighing on my side was her knowledge that I am a very defensive driver and have logged thousands of miles on the road on a bicycle and understood the two-wheels versus four-wheels challenge. It also helped that the kids were older, and we were financially secure. She insisted, however, that I made sure my will was filled out.

I took the MSF course so I would learn the right way to ride and found that riding a motorcycle was joyfully similar to riding a bicycle. Luckily, my friends who rode sport-touring bikes guided me to good gear and a used Suzuki GS500F. I had considered a cruiser, but it just wasn't me.

The GS500 was wonderful. It proved very forgiving of mistakes in throttle control and cornering lines. Like a smart horse, it just seemed to know what I wanted. Between commuting and weekends, I rode that bike 7,000 miles in six months.

On overnight trips, however, I bumped up against the motorcycle's carrying-capacity limitations. Bungee-cording all my stuff to the back of the bike got to be unwieldy. The GS500's suspension system, lack of wind protection, and passing limitations on the slab also left something to be desired. When the weather turned colder, I bought an FJR1300, which I felt able to handle by then. With the addition of heated gear, I rode every day possible.

I met many riders through the local meet-up groups and developed friendships with about a dozen riders who try to do a ride-eat-ride every weekend and longer trips in the late spring and early fall. For me, riding is the perfect combination of the satisfaction of ever-developing skill and experience and personal freedom and camaraderie.

I have a Roadcrafter suit and heated gear so I am well equipped for weather conditions and protected against possible road rash. The bike has side bags and a Givi top case, so I have plenty of room for a week's travel if I need it. What

## Transporting a Bike

If you have a pickup truck or access to a trailer suitable for hauling a motorcycle, you can save some time by putting in a few long travel days on the interstate, hauling the bike to a desired ride start point. Most motorcycle retailers sell ramps for loading a bike into the bed of a pickup truck; the ramps aren't overly expensive. And you can rent or even buy a trailer suitable for hauling a motorcycle if you decide to use this transport method often. Some companies will ship your motorcycle to a location for you, but the expense and

Eric Lader, on his second motorcycle, the FJR1300, preparing for longer travels

I don't know is how my posterior will take to 500-mile days. The most I have ridden in a day is 250 miles. My first longer trip will be to visit my kid (500 miles each way), and I'll see how that goes.

I do miss the spontaneity of a lightweight bike. I am thinking about getting a 250cc, 350-pound dual-sport for commuting on nice days and for trying my hand at some tame dirt trails.

## Consider This

One morning, while taking a ride through northern Georgia's lovely, curving mountain roads, I noticed that I couldn't seem to get in the riding groove—that my lines through curves were off, and that entry speeds didn't seem right. I was aware that my concentration and focus were not what they should have been. I kept thinking to myself, "What is the problem today?" I realized that I had jumped on the bike that morning after having two cups of coffee and no breakfast, and I probably wasn't thinking as clearly because of it.

Sure enough, a stop for a decent breakfast made all the difference. I was more alert, more relaxed, and riding more smoothly. I rode better for the rest of the morning because I took a break to nourish my body—and my brain. Running on empty may not be as big a factor when driving a car, but when riding, anything that affects reaction and response time not only lowers the enjoyment level of riding but also threatens the safe operation of the bike.

complication of this method probably make it less practical for short- to medium-length tours.

I have ridden the bike from start to finish on most of my touring vacations. On one summer vacation to Florida's Panhandle, however, where my wife and her family had rented a house for a week, I used a motorcycle ramp to put my bike on the bed of my truck so I could take it along. Doing this, I had the advantage of being able to pack gear for ocean fun (snorkeling equipment, a skim board, swim fins) that I couldn't have taken had I ridden the bike (no room to pack swim fins in the saddlebags!). Having the bike available gave me the chance to change the focus of several days of the vacation from beach activities to day-long riding opportunities, when I could tour the natural and unpopulated areas of Florida along the Gulf of Mexico.

# Flying There and Renting

Flying to your starting point and renting a bike is probably the easiest, most convenient, and least time-consuming method for touring an area far from home—though it's certainly not the least expensive. Rental rates for full-size touring bikes and touring cruisers range from $100 a day to more than $175 a day. Cost varies depending on what you rent and where you rent and if you add the rental company's insurance. Your own motorcycle insurance may cover rentals (check with your agent), but concerns about damaging a rented bike may make paying for the rental company's full-coverage insurance, just for the peace of mind, worthwhile.

Another advantage of renting a motorcycle is the ability to reserve a specific kind of bike. You can get a real feel for how it would be to own that Harley, Honda, or BMW that you have always thought about purchasing.

Other benefits of renting include avoiding the complications of shipping your own bike to a starting point and saving your bike from the wear and tear of the ride (you put the miles on the rental bike, not your own). Many rental agencies will also pick you up and return you to either an airport or a hotel as part of the deal. Some rentals include a helmet and rainsuit, so you don't have to transport all of your bulky gear. Don't assume that they are included, however—ask. If helmets are indeed included, find out what types are offered; rental helmets are often the half-helmet variety. You want full protection.

In 2002, while still living in the Atlanta area, my wife, Lora, and I planned a five-day motorcycling vacation out West. We would travel from Salt Lake City up to Yellowstone National Park, then west through

**Streetmasters Advice from *Walt Fulton***

# I See Them, So Why Can't They See Me?

*Inattentional blindness* may be a major factor in intersection collisions involving cars and motorcycles. Never heard the term before? Then it's time to become familiar with it, because understanding inattentional blindness could save your life. Marc Green, a human factors expert and author of the article "Inattentional Blindness and Conspicuity" (see www.visualexpert.com/Resources/inattentionalblindness.html) suggests that this condition and its often catastrophic results are more prevalent than imagined. Think of inattentional blindness as looking but not seeing.

Green says that four factors affect inattentional blindness: mental workload, expectation (that is, what we expect to see versus what's actually there), conspicuity, and capacity (to pay attention). You can have an effect on two: conspicuity and capacity.

You can enhance your conspicuity (in Marc Green's words, "the ability to capture attention") to other road users by wearing riding gear that contrasts with the background "noise." High-visibility (for daytime) vests with retroreflective material (for nighttime) should help to do the job. Retroreflective stickers on the saddlebags, fork legs, rear fender, and even your helmet will improve

Retroreflective material on this rider's gear helps to keep her visible to drivers, which keeps her safer.

your conspicuity to others at night, too. Green also points out that lights that flicker are more likely to be noticed; modulating headlights and brake lights do just that.

Don't make the mistake of relying on loud pipes to gain a driver's

My wife (then-fiancée), Lora, and I flew to Salt Lake City and rented a Gold Wing for a tour of the West, including the Tetons (*above*). Renting made the trip easy.

attention. In many situations—as when a car is about to make a left turn into you—the driver will not hear you. Loud pipes aren't the answer; being seen is.

Clearly, a rider's or a driver's capacity to pay attention is reduced under the influence of drugs or alcohol and when the rider/driver is fatigued. Riding under the influence or when tired are two surefire ways to quickly become a statistic on two wheels. Don't do it. And be on the lookout for cars being driven erratically. Give them a wide berth.

"Attentional capacity is also a function of experience," Green states. When you are a new rider, a task as complex as motorcycling requires you to focus most of your attention on controlling the motorcycle; you have little attention left over to handle important tasks

such as noticing signal lights, other traffic, pedestrians, and corners. Become very familiar with all of the controls and how to use them by developing muscle memory before you put yourself in complex riding situations.

While we're at it, let's take a look at the other two factors so that you understand what they mean to you. *Mental workload* is a technical phrase that refers to spreading ourselves thin by focusing on too many things at one time. Examples for a driver would be tuning the radio, trying to find the bagel that just dropped on the floor, hollering at the kids in the back seat, or talking on a cell phone. (If a driver's doing all of this at the same time, that's not mental workload, it's mental overload!)

Expectation has to do with what you have grown to expect under

certain conditions or in certain areas. For instance, a motorcyclist who is riding home late at night when the traffic is light, as he often does, approaches an intersection where he has never seen a left-turning vehicle. Tonight there is one, but he doesn't see it because he doesn't expect it. Familiarity with the area has caused inattentional blindness. By contrast, when motorcyclists ride in unfamiliar areas, they tend to be more attentive.

It's your responsibility to make certain that you stand out and are noticed, that you become familiar with the operation of your bike, and that you stay alert. And remember that you, too, can be the one experiencing inattentional blindness—it's not just the other guy—so be sure to continually get the big picture. (See Get the Big Picture, page 85.)

Montana and Idaho and back to Salt Lake. Having taken a short test ride on an older model Gold Wing many months before, I wanted to experience what it was like to really travel on one. Renting one was the perfect opportunity to combine a trip in the West with the experience of riding a Gold Wing for several days. It was a fairly simple matter to find a place that rented Gold Wings in Salt Lake City.

We flew out of Atlanta on a Friday night, arrived in Salt Lake City, and got a hotel room near the rental location. Having gotten there by ten o'clock Saturday morning, we were traveling north by noon. The Gold Wing we rented was brand new, with only 5 miles on the odometer. (This is another advantage of

renting, as most motorcycles in rental fleets are new or nearly new, with low mileage and a high level of maintenance.) The Gold Wing ended up being a dream motorcycle, and our trip a first-rate touring experience. When we returned to Salt Lake five days later, we turned the bike in with 1,532 miles on the odometer (that's an average of about 300 miles per day), paid the balance of the bill, and took a plane home the next morning. The entire rental process was a smooth one from start to finish.

## ≫ A Rider's Tale
# Debbie's Story: A Sense of Freedom

Debbie Monk and her Dyna Low Rider

At the time I purchased my first bike, I was forty-three and had no clue as to whether I could rise to this challenge. Yet I was now the owner of a 2005 Dyna Low Rider and would rather have chewed my arm off than admit to anyone I was a bit afraid. I had decided to begin street riding, as, back in the day (and no, not in the covered-wagon days), I had ridden dirt bikes and had a lot of fun doing it.

My kids thought I had taken leave of my senses, but I explained that I couldn't afford an RV, so this was the next best way to travel the countryside, seeing the sights, meeting new people, and expanding my horizons.

This was, without a doubt, one of the best decisions I have ever made. It has not been without its trials, however. I have had to learn to ride in some difficult situations that have tested my resolve, my commitment to the sport, and my abilities as a rider. I approach each ride with caution and joy, and I have learned to love the pre-trip jitters I sometimes get—they keep me on the lookout.

My 2005 Dyna Low Rider has been a faithful friend, one that has never let me down on the road. That steel horse certainly helped

me keep my sanity through some rough times in my life. I can laugh about getting lost in a strange town, and I don't mind the strange looks I get from people who can't get used to the idea of a woman riding a motorcycle. In addition, I've met some great people in my journeys.

I encourage other women to step out of their comfort zones and live the reality of a biker woman. And do it not on the back of someone else's bike, but on their own bikes. You enjoy a sense of independence and freedom when you are in charge.

Two motorcyclists travel through Canada's Yukon. Many companies offer organized tours in the United States, Canada, and abroad.

# Taking an Organized Tour

For those who prefer to travel with a group and have others take care of the details, there are many tour companies that will do just that. Organized touring companies will do the planning for you and arrange for your lodging; they may also provide a chase vehicle for luggage and bring along extra motorcycles should mechanical problems put bikes out of commission. With such companies, you can ride in different regions of North America or cross the ocean to explore Germany's Black Forest, ride the Alps' challenging switchback roads, or go on an African motorcycle safari.

Some touring companies offer much more than other companies do. For example, one business that features motorcycle tours through India and the Himalayas provides, in its all-inclusive price, comfortable accommodations with breakfast and dinner; motorcycles with fuel, oil, and spares; air, train, and car transfers during the tour; English-speaking ride leaders and support crew; and backup support vehicles.

I know many people who love organized touring for their motorcycle traveling, as this method allows them to journey to places they would never have visited on their own.

Beautiful sandstone formations, canyons, and cliffs characterize much of the West, including Utah's Capitol Reef National Park (*above*). All that open land, however, means a lot of distance between fuel stops, so be prepared and plan accordingly.

# Going West

I f you're from the East Coast and considering touring in the western United States, understand that the landscape can be very different from what you are used to. Maps of many states west of the Mississippi show some very sparsely populated areas, and this is not because the cartographers were too lazy to put in the details. In some cases, you may have to go more than 100 miles between towns to find opportunities for refueling and a place to stay the night. Although bikes and gas tanks seem to be getting larger every year (with a corresponding increase in traveling range), be aware that any motorcycle that has

**Streetmasters Advice from *Walt Fulton***

## Staying Hydrated

Riding season for most of us is during the warmer times of the year. Because of that, there is an often overlooked but critical issue that we need to be aware of: proper hydration. As much as we hate interrupting our fun rides with biological breaks, it is extremely important to drink ample water and/or sports drinks with the proper electrolytes and minerals.

This CamelBak hydration system attached to the rider's back allows him to carry a supply of water, which he taps into through a drinking tube attached to the unit.

To have your body break down due to dehydration is serious business. Dehydration is an insidious condition that develops quickly and has grave and even deadly consequences if not treated quickly. And it's not just heat that causes dehydration. As you ride through the wind, you tend to dry out.

When dehydration begins to occur, your body sends subtle signals that you must pay close attention to and immediately heed. If you are thirsty, which is the first sign, you are already heading down the dehydration path. Do *not* ignore this sign.

Stop and start drinking. If you don't, you will get even more dehydrated, which often makes you feel slightly nauseous and light-headed.

When you get to this stage, you *must pull over immediately* and drink some water! Once you've reached this point, you aren't far away from losing consciousness. The last thing you want to be doing when your body collapses is riding down the road at speed. Here's the good news: water, electrolytes, and rest will rejuvenate your body.

In warm and dry weather, a hydration system (such as the CamelBak) is a good investment; it'll help you maintain the steady intake of fluids into your system as you ride. This is even more critical if you wear a mesh jacket (or worse—no jacket), because the wind will suck the moisture out of your unprotected body. Be aware, as well, that downing coffee, tea, and other caffeinated drinks actually dehydrates you more. So after that first cup of joe in the morning, do your body a favor and switch to friendlier fluids.

a range of fewer than 200 miles in a tankful should be refilled at any town that has a gas station. In addition, routes that appear fairly straightforward may go over or through mountain ranges (this may also apply, to a lesser extent, to mountainous areas on the East Coast), extending the time you need to go from point A to point B. To avoid surprises, get maps that have topographical detail of the areas you will be riding through. In many cases, an opportunity to ride through spectacular terrain is exactly why you would want to take a specific route, but you need to plan for the extra time it may take.

Although cell-phone coverage may be spottier in less populated areas, carrying a cell phone and a travel guide along with a GPS that can display hotel and gas-station location information can help you find lodging and fuel when needed. And while you may be less likely to choose to travel by motorcycle in colder months, high elevations in the western United States can still surprise you with some very cold temperatures in the summer season—even an August snowfall (it has happened to me!).

## Finding Information on Roads and Routes

Websites catering to motorcycle-specific roads and routes (that is, scenic highways and "the road less traveled") are becoming more plentiful, making it easier to plan routes that get you off of the interstates and freeways. In addition to listing some of the better motorcycle-riding roads, many of the sites feature postings from riders that give additional information on specific routes, and include information on places to stay, photographs of roads, and maps with mileage information about roads and routes. Here are a few:

- BestBikingRoads.com (www.bestbikingroads .com): this site has information on roads and routes throughout Europe, North and South America, Asia, Australia, and Africa.

- MadMaps (www.madmaps.com); Motorcycle Roads.US (www.motorcycleroads.us); Motorcycle Roads.com (www.motorcycleroads.com): these sites have information on roads and routes throughout the United States.

---

**Streetmasters Advice from *Walt Fulton***

# Blowin' in the Wind

The iconic song by Bob Dylan tells us that "the answer is blowin' in the wind." As motorcyclists, we're always blowing in the wind, but when the wind begins to blow us around, things can get exciting or downright uncomfortable. In different parts of the country and at different times of the year, strong seasonal winds can create control issues that may cause some of us to keep our bikes in the garage.

Typically, wind speed is measured in knots (nautical miles per hour), but to make it simple, we'll use miles per hour here. Wind speed approaching 30 to 40 miles per hour shouldn't be much of a problem for most riders, even when the wind is coming at the rider at a 90-degree angle. A gentle and constant press on the handlebar toward the direction of the wind will lean your bike into the wind and keep you traveling in your intended direction.

At higher wind speeds, more handlebar press is needed, and

the bike must lean even more to counteract the wind's force. Riding for hours in a steady wind can

Many other websites provide information on motorcycling roads and routes worldwide as well as ones with information specific to one continent or a particular country. Just do an Internet search for "motorcycle routes and roads" or similar search terms and add the location where you are planning to ride. In addition, literally dozens of motorcycling books cater specifically to touring roads and locations, and any bookstore or online outlet will have them available.

Two of the volumes that I have enjoyed the most are *Great American Motorcycle Tours* by Gary McKechnie (Avalon Travel Publishing, 2002), and *Extreme Twisties— Southeastern USA* by William Long (L & A Publishing, 1999).

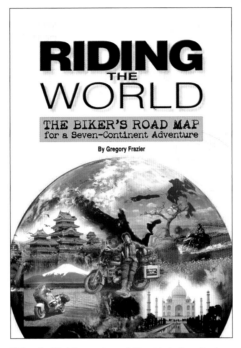

*Riding the World* is a motorcyclist's guide by Greg Frazier, who's circumnavigated the globe five times by himself.

Long's *Extreme Twisties* is a book of short tours and loop rides in the southeastern United States that features small maps and information about the rides and the roads. When I lived in the area, I always kept a copy of the book in my saddlebag. *Extreme Twisties* is now out of print, but copies can be found through used-book vendors online.

If you are seriously contemplating circumnavigating the globe by motorcycle, you may want to pick up a copy of *Adventure Motorcycling Handbook: Worldwide Motorcycling Route and Planning Guide* by Chris Scott (Trailblazer Publications, 5th ed., 2006). This highly regarded book is packed with practical information from initial planning to the best roads and routes to travel.

It's better not to be riding in severe winds, but you should know how to counter the effects of wind before you go long distances.

and even tucking in to reduce the wind's effect on the lever arm— your upper body above the seat. This should allow you to keep the bike more upright.

The situation gets more serious when you are fighting wind gusts wind. One moment, you're riding straight down the road, and the next you've been pushed across two lanes. This is when keeping your upper body relaxed is essential. Staying relaxed will allow you to execute precise steering input

that will keep you in your lane of travel, ensure that you arrive at your destination less tired, and make the trip a safer one. If you tense up your arms and shoulders, you won't be able to react quickly, smoothly, and precisely to a wind gust.

In addition, though it may seem counterintuitive, try to ride as quickly as you can safely manage. The slower you ride, the greater the ability of the wind to alter your direction.

Practice these techniques when the gusts are gentle to gain your confidence and develop your precision handlebar input.

be a tiring task, so you may want to try shifting your weight into the wind by sliding over on the seat

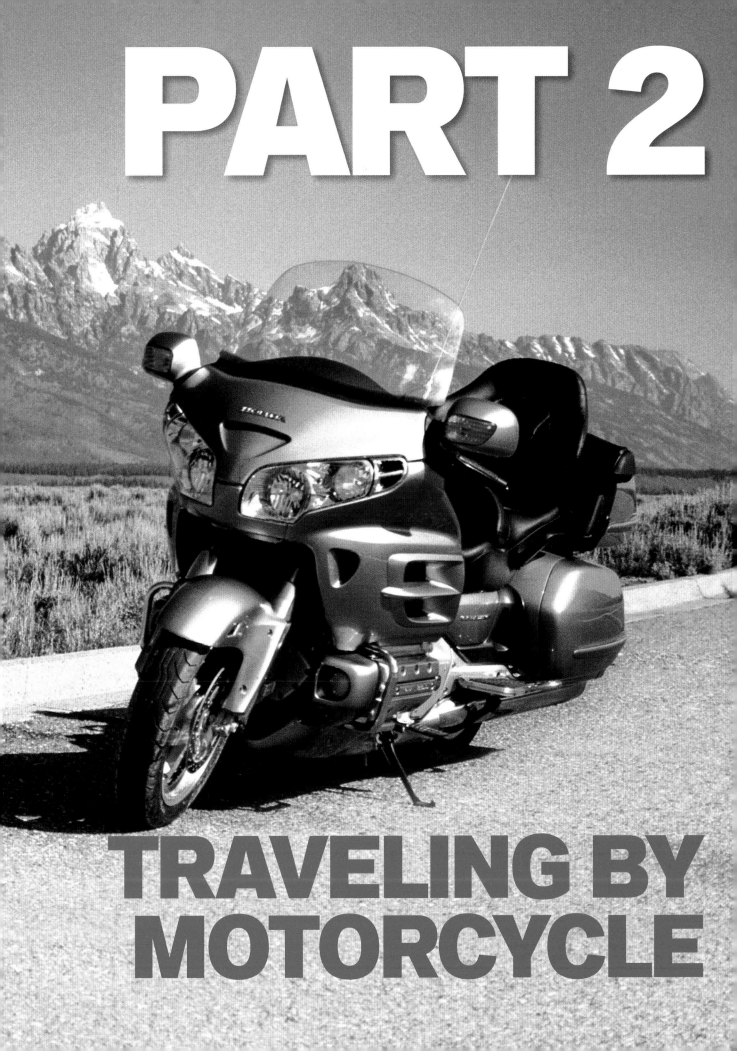

# PART 2

# TRAVELING BY MOTORCYCLE

# THE REAL FLORIDA

>>> This story is a ride to Florida that covered more of the west coast area. It was the first travel article that I wrote with the intention of attempting to sell it to a magazine. The magazine I submitted it to was called *Motorcycle Tour and Cruiser* (later called *Road-bike*). The magazine's editor accepted the article for publication (you can imagine my excitement!), and an edited version of it appeared in the August 1999 issue.

This was my first published article in a national magazine, and it turned out to be the start of an entirely new direction in my life. What follows is the original story (as I submitted it), with updated information in brackets.

Left: Pelicans take flight from a Florida jetty.
Above: The Destin coast on the Gulf of Mexico

# Atlanta to the Panhandle

I have never been one to plan vacations. Rather than setting an itinerary, I usually start with a general destination and outline of what I want to do and avoid specifics except when necessary. Daily life is usually about schedules and deadlines, so I like my travel plans to be more off-the-cuff. Having decided that this year's vacation would be a motorcycle trip into Florida, I made no definite plans other than to spend Memorial Day weekend with friends and family in the town of Destin, on the Gulf of Mexico, and to visit family and friends in Fort Myers the following weekend. I had an open week and could ride wherever I wanted to and do whatever I liked. The motorcycle I was traveling on was a Suzuki VS1400 Intruder. I had purchased the bike new a few months before, and with 2,500 miles on the odometer, I was thoroughly comfortable on the bike and ready for the ten-day riding trip in the Sunshine State.

The vacation began Friday, May 22, when I left my place in an Atlanta suburb at about noon. [Although published in 1999, this story was written in 1998, when the Memorial Day holiday fell on May 25.] I would be traveling during the hottest part of the day, but I wanted to avoid the Memorial Day holiday rush hour traffic. With the El Niño–influenced weather of the summer, I'd be experiencing 90-degree temperatures and high humidity, although no rain was forecast for the weekend in the Florida Panhandle area.

Meeting friends and family that night in Destin meant I had to take the most direct route to the Florida Panhandle, which is Interstate 85 South out of Atlanta to Montgomery, Alabama, then US Route 331 South across the Alabama border into Florida. By midafternoon, I was winding my way through the southern part of Montgomery, following signs to US 331. Breaks for bottled water, to fill up, and to check the map were my only stops. I looked forward to getting off the interstate for the rest of the day and onto Highway 331, heading toward the cooler

Catamarans and beachgoers parked on the white-sand beaches at Destin

Riding east on Florida 30 (now West County Highway 30A) to the town of Seaside, I came across Big Redfish Lake and stopped to take photographs.

sea breezes off the Florida gulf. It was hot—uncomfortably so—and not optimum riding weather. (If you are from cooler climes and considering a motorcycle tour south in the summer, take heed—drink lots of water and wear a ventilated helmet and safety clothing. The heat and humidity will wear you down. If you can work it out, plan to ride in the morning and early evening hours and spend midday on the beach. You'll get a lot more out of the trip.)

Highway 331 in Alabama is a typical rural "two-laner" that runs north and south with the occasional sweeping curve and a few stretches in need of repaving. Old farmhouses, deserted gas stations, and abandoned shacks dot the road, contributing to the highway's scenic quality. Unfortunately, 331 is

also a favorite north-south truck route, so your forward momentum can be slowed by traffic, requiring the occasional passing maneuver. Roads like this, however, definitely beat interstate travel. Although it was hot, trees overhanging the road provided welcome shade from the afternoon sun, and the abandoned buildings on the side of the road offered a timeless backdrop for photographs.

By 5:30 p.m., I had crossed the Choctawhatchee Bay and was closing in on Santa Rosa Beach. It had been a pleasant surprise that holiday traffic was relatively light. The last leg of my first day's ride was on US Route 98, heading west, and by 6:30 p.m., I was knocking on the door of the condominium in Destin, where I would spend the holiday weekend.

with a sign reading "Beaches" and made a spur-of-the-moment decision to go exploring. (As Yogi Berra says, "When you come to a fork in the road, take it.") The long U-shaped road led to Seaside, a thriving town on the Gulf with pastel blue and pink beach houses that probably sell for a small fortune. Throughout this area and surrounding the town are state-protected sand dune parks, saltwater marshes, and bird sanctuaries, all contributing to an atmosphere that is much like Florida was before development—the natural Florida.

I stopped at the trendy little Pizza Bar restaurant in Seaside and ordered a slice of its *breakfast pizza* with a melon cup and coffee. In Seaside, *trendy* means overpriced and a wait staff that speaks in a reverent white-glove-establishment tone usually reserved for four-star dining. ("In addition to our breakfast pizza, may we recommend our melon cup with kiwi fruit and cantaloupe garnished with parsley?") Jeez, it's just scrambled eggs and coffee, you know? OK, it was vacation, so I chalked it up to being part of the experience.

A bit overdressed for beach weather in my denim and riding boots, I moved outside to a table where I could feel the sea breeze and have a direct line of sight to my motorcycle. The bike has leather

As most of us who live in the southeastern United States know, Destin is a smaller resort town located about seven miles east of Fort Walton Beach. The town has great restaurants, clubs, hotels, and condominiums, most within walking distance of the white-sand beaches of the Gulf. The riding in the area is largely unchallenging, as it is relatively flat with few curves, but the ocean scenery is beautiful and more than makes up for the geography. In my opinion, Destin is a much nicer place to spend a weekend than Panama City Beach, which has more of the glitz and tourist-trap feel to it.

On Saturday morning, I got on the bike to do a little exploring. Taking Highway 98 about 20 miles east of Destin, I came upon a road

The VS1400 at an abandoned grocery store and gas station on US 331

saddlebags, so I like to keep an eye on things whenever possible. Generally speaking, people don't bother the motorcycle, but there are always those few individuals whose larcenous intentions can ruin a vacation.

While I was eating, a driver of a delivery truck backed into the sand-covered parking lot next to my bike, going at what seemed like 15 miles per hour. He slammed on the brakes, stopping within a few feet of the bike's rear tire. A cloud of dust kicked up by the truck settled slowly on the bike. None too happy about this, I got up to investigate. A wiry sunburned man jumped out the driver's seat and ran to the back door of the truck. He opened the door with a full-armed swing, slamming it against the back of the truck, once again barely missing my motorcycle. Slightly annoyed, I asked if he would like me to move the bike. He had that ruddy, leathery complexion that comes from too many beers on too many hot days, and he seemed oblivious to my irritation. I got the feeling that the guy was not exactly "all there," so while he was telling me that the bike was "just fine where it is," I opted to roll the motorcycle an additional 10 feet away. Then I finished my breakfast and rode a circuitous route that got me back to the condo at about 2 p.m.

For the rest of the weekend, the bike remained parked, covered, and locked. The days on the beach and nights in the clubs, along with the occasional imbibing that went with that agenda, meant that transportation was best left to others, so I enjoyed the weekend riding with family and friends as a passenger. Memorial Day weekend in Destin is what you would expect it to be—lots of sun, seafood restaurants, and great bands in little nightclubs, where you party until the early hours, then start all over again the next day.

A deserted patch of beach at St. Joseph Peninsula State Park (*far left*); a group of gulls socialize on the beach.

## Eastward along the Gulf Coast

**M**onday morning, I continued my trip on US Route 98, which is one of the nicest rides this state has to offer. The highway stretches some 300 miles from Pensacola to south of Tallahassee, winding along Florida's coast and within sight of the Gulf of Mexico for much of its length. Other than the town of Panama City, populated areas consist of mostly blink-and-you-miss-them towns with little or no traffic. The highway has its share of easy curves that make the ride interesting but not challenging, and the picturesque small towns and stretches of undeveloped coastline make for excellent sightseeing as you ride. Although it ate up time, I couldn't resist the numerous opportunities to stop and take photographs where the road and the view were spectacular.

The scenery included lots of undeveloped coast with water coming almost to the road's edge, gulls perched on a skiff tied to a short pier on the water, local harbors with thirty-year-old fishing boats and fishermen working in the rigging, and old seaside houses on stilts along the shore.

Fishing boats at harbor near Apalachicola, Florida

At a stop for gas at a convenience store west of Apalachicola, I noticed a lovely young woman standing in the store's open doorway talking to a much older man behind the counter. As I was walking into the store, she turned to leave. She smiled at me, and I smiled back and said hello. I got some bottled water, and at the counter, I remarked about the lovely lady and asked the older man if she was his daughter. His squinty-eyed reply was "She's my wife," and the conversation died that very moment. I smiled, said thank you,

Highway 98 sweeps in easy curves along the Gulf Coast of Florida, making for a leisurely and scenic ride.

and moved quickly. I decided then and there not to ask too many questions for the rest of the trip.

After riding through Tyndall Air Force Base on Highway 98, just south of Port St. Joe at a town called Oak Grove—which I wouldn't have known existed except for a small roadside sign—I detoured off the highway to take a coastal road, State Road 30 [now SR 30A]. This road led through marshland and along the water's edge to County Road 30 East, which takes you to St. Joseph Peninsula State Park (see page 115), an undeveloped strip of land with few amenities, except for public restrooms and showers for park patrons. The camping areas are set up for tents and small RVs, and the whole park is unspoiled white sand dunes, beach, and turquoise water. If I had been camping, this was the place I would have stayed the night. The receipt from the park entrance read "The Real Florida." [Update: There are now eight cabins available for rent on the bay side of the park. For information on the park, check out www.floridastateparks.org/stjoseph/.]

That is the beauty of traveling by motorcycle. If I had been driving a car this week, I probably would have been traveling on I-something to somewhere, and I would have driven right by the entire area, never knowing what was here.

## Off the Panhandle and Toward the East Coast

I followed County Road 30 East back to SR 30 [SR 30A], took a right, and rode the remainder of the road east back to Highway 98. South of Tallahassee, the highway begins to move inland, away from the coast. At the town of Perry, I picked up ALT 27 (Alternate US 27) going east toward Gainesville, and by then, the scenery had changed considerably from the coastal areas. Straight stretches of road with the occasional wetlands were the routine now, and the route was completely devoid of traffic.

The weather forecast was for continued clear skies, and although it was better than riding in the rain, it was hot and the wetland environment contributed to a higher than the normally high humidity. Without the cooling effects from the Gulf, not

even a riding speed of 65 miles per hour offered much cooling relief in the humid air. With the stops for photographs, fuel, and liquid refreshments, it turned into a nine-hour riding day. Near 8 p.m., I arrived in Gainesville and found a hotel with a pizza-and-beer joint right across the street and checked in. After a cool shower, I walked over to the restaurant

I passed many Florida wetlands such as these on the way to the east coast.

for a couple of slices of pizza and an equal number of beers and called it a night.

On Tuesday morning, I took State Route 20 out of Gainesville to SR 207, headed toward St. Augustine and Florida's east coast. The riding in this area was a bit . . . uninspiring, I guess you'd say. It was mostly straight stretches of two-lane highway with the occasional country store or abandoned shack on the side of the road to break up the monotony. High clouds in the late morning blocked the strongest rays of the sun, cooling the temperatures somewhat, and the weekday morning's light traffic made for a comfortable, easy ride. At St. Augustine, I encountered the traffic and tourists that I had been lucky enough to avoid so far on the trip. Well, it had to happen sooner or later, as this city is a prime tourist location, after all. I pulled into a parking lot to take some quick photographs of Flagler College (a beautiful building) and then continued east toward the coast. Within thirty minutes, I had made my way out to SR A1A and headed south toward Daytona Beach.

Once a luxury hotel, built in the Spanish style, Flagler College is considered one of the most beautiful campuses in the United States.

## St. Augustine to Daytona Beach

**B**etween St. Augustine and Ormond Beach, A1A is straight and flat, but the ocean view on most of this highway makes the ride a nice one. Farther south, much of the waterside real estate has been bought up and filled with hotels, condos, beachside bars, and restaurants, but up here, large stretches of waterfront are still undeveloped, with just bridges elevated over open spans of blue water and sea oats gracing white sand. There's something about seeing these colors that brings a settled and peaceful feeling to the spirit. I made a quick stop and walked out onto an overpass to photograph an inlet to the Intracoastal Waterway, where less than a dozen people occupied a huge expanse of beach.

A little north of Ormond Beach, I stopped at a beachside bar and grill for lunch. In front of the restaurant, an older man occupied a canvas-covered four-post stand with a sign in front that read "Valet Parking." This struck me as odd, as there were only a handful of cars parked on the sand around the place, with no need for someone to jockey parking places on a Tuesday afternoon. I surmised that he was a beach entrepreneur of sorts—an enterprising but laid-back type who could sit on the beach all day, have a beer or two, get a buck from each patron, and collect enough to make ends meet (an enviable lifestyle to some, I guess). He directed me to a parking place and, helpfully, found a flat rock to put the kickstand on. I said thanks and went inside.

Although there are occasional exceptions, when I am in traveling mode, I usually don't make long stops to take in tourist attractions or events that keep me away from the bike for too long. On this motorcycle, everything I bring with me is either strapped to the bike or stored in the leather throw-over saddlebags, leaving my belongings pretty much unprotected. [Update: I have a bike with locking saddlebags now!] Most often, this makes enjoying longer stops away from the bike more difficult. I was

This is the photograph of me, the VS1400, and the beachside bar and grill taken by the enterprising "beach valet."

This is a view of Ormond Beach on A1A near sunset. North of Daytona, the beaches are less developed, and traffic levels are low.

glad that, in this case, there was someone watching things while I was away from the motorcycle.

Out in the back of the restaurant was a long expanse of deserted beach (not unusual on a mid-week afternoon). Again, I saw some opportunities for good photographs—an unoccupied beach umbrella and chair at the water's edge, sailboats on the water—and I stood out on the back patio taking photos while I waited for lunch.

After lunch, I got the beach valet to take a photo of me in front of the bike, stuffed a few bucks in his tip jar, and resumed the journey south. Around Daytona, A1A became a mess of traffic; in an effort to get around it, I rode west, away from the coast. At US 1, I turned south again, and after a few miles, I saw a sign pointing east that read "To A1A." Wanting to get back to riding the coast, I took the road and went about 10 miles east and south before seeing another sign saying "Road Ends." It was then that I found out that A1A dead-ends at an upscale residential community at Ponce Inlet. Wonderful. If

there was a sign anywhere on this stretch indicating that the road was ending, I never saw it. OK, another lesson learned: stop and consult a map when you find yourself riding unfamiliar roads.

In general, the east coast of Florida is nice riding, but in this man's humble opinion, the roads become a bit of a mess in the Daytona area. I decided to detour around the entire area and ride I-95 South to make up the time lost to my directional miscues. At Titusville, I took SR 50 toward Orlando, and when I arrived there, I decided to treat myself to a nice room at a Radisson Hotel for the night. At dinner that evening, I contemplated the week's travels thus far and realized that I was starting to rack up miles getting from place to place without fully enjoying what I was doing. I decided to try to make up for this the following morning by getting back to the west coast to ride the coastal roads south to Fort Myers.

Overleaf: The Intracoastal Waterway comprises a series of artificial canals and waterways connected to aid in shipping and transportation.

I stopped for a photograph of this Spanish-style courtyard door on SR A1A, south of St. Augustine. Punta Gorda had similar sites.

## Central Florida to the West Coast

On Wednesday morning, the view to the west was overcast and gray. Orlando was still clear, but I could see that riding toward the coast meant riding through rain, so to avoid the inclement weather, I chose roads south through the middle of the state with the idea of making my way west later in the day. US 27 South to I-4 West seemed the best route, then SR 60 West to US 17 South leading to the coastal town Punta Gorda. It was a race to beat the rain, and for I thought I was going to lose, as I got an occasional spattering of water on the windshield, but once I turned onto US 17, the rain clouds disappeared.

OK, I thought, let's tour central Florida. Well, that's why I avoid itineraries on motorcycle trips—I have to be prepared to improvise. Midstate Florida below I-4 is wide open and flat, with great expanses of farmland and savannas, and with older small towns spread out along most routes.

After a long ride, US 17 ended at US 41 in Punta Gorda. The clouds were gone and the sky was blue and the sunshine intense. Punta Gorda is a great-looking little town, with many Spanish-style buildings featuring arch-crowned doorways and

are smaller and more peaceful, without the traffic problems, the intense rush, or the "big city" attitude. There are still large areas of undeveloped land where a moderate income can buy a decent-size piece of property and a house at a reasonable price. The beaches are clean and not crowded and, unlike the other side of the state, devoid of high-rise hotels and condominiums covering every possible inch of waterfront. I hope I am wrong, but it is my guess that both developers and area governments view southeast Florida as played out, and within another ten years they will begin developing this area as the next Florida resort gold mine, complete with an ever-expanding tax base. [Update: Whether due to conscientious zoning practices, the slow economy of the past several years, or both, southwest Florida, I am glad to report, is still a very picturesque and conscientiously developed area.]

A sailboat on Fort Myers Beach

storefronts with wrought iron gates and railings. Some of the buildings are painted a coral or light blue color, giving the town that tropical feeling associated with much of Florida—very refreshing to the eye. I rode down Highway 41 South to take it all in, with the idea of getting a room on Fort Myers Beach and exploring the area for the remainder of the week.

In the late sixties and early seventies, my family lived in southeast Florida (in the North Miami area), and Florida's west coast reminds me of what the east coast was like when I was a kid. The towns

Arriving in the Fort Myers area, I rode out to Sanibel Island to see if I might find a reasonably priced room available anywhere in the area. Out here is perfect Florida living, with stilt houses, low-key hotels, and great restaurants, many with an unobstructed view of the Gulf of Mexico. Because the summer months are actually the off season in

Florida, I thought I might find something at a more affordable price. No such luck. The going rate was a bit of a budget buster, so I headed back to Fort Myers Beach. There I got a room at a hotel on the beach that was within walking distance of the area's restaurants and clubs, which meant riding the bike for meals and entertainment or to run errands would be an option rather than a necessity. I made a few phone calls to family and friends, and later that evening, one of my brothers and his family came out to have dinner with me at a local restaurant.

On Thursday, an intermittent light rain put a "damper" on riding plans, but the day off allowed me to enjoy more time with family (with another brother and his family) and some time on the beach.

Friday morning was clear with strong sunshine, and a high-school girlfriend, Karen, came for a visit. Although both of us had grown up in South Florida, neither of us had seen this area until now, and we planned to ride out on Sanibel Island for the day. She didn't have a helmet, so I figured I would call a motorcycle shop to see if I could rent one for the day. A quick check in the yellow pages found no motorcycle shops in the local area, but there was a place that rented scooters on the beach. I called them to ask about renting a helmet, and the woman who answered said that they didn't have helmets to rent, but that I could borrow hers for the day. Amazing. She told me her name and said I should ask for her when I got there. I rode over to the shop, and she just smiled and handed me the helmet.

Surprisingly, this is one of the few photos I have taken of Sanibel Island.

No ID, nothing to sign, just "Here, have a great day."

And we did. Sanibel Island is really something. It is flat as a pancake and only inches above sea level. The small island is full of native palm trees and tropical plants, and any structures built there seem designed to blend in with the surrounding scenery. Trees overhang the minimal two-lane road that snakes through Sanibel and its neighbor Captiva Island, and we wound through the curves at a leisurely pace, taking it all in.

On these islands, there are no high rises, condominiums, or any of the beach overdevelopment often found in other places in this state. Houses on stilts face the Gulf of Mexico, and small grocery stores and restaurants are set back from the road and surrounded by trees and native plants, giving the entire area an unspoiled real Florida feel. We stopped at a small coral-colored grocery store to buy a couple of lottery tickets (well, someone has to win), and as we rode, music from our high-school days played on headphones under our helmets. It was a perfect day.

A cabbage palm tree grows on the Gulf of Mexico near Apalachicola, Florida.

# Florida to Home

On Saturday, I packed and loaded the bike. My brothers and their families and my friend Karen met me for breakfast, and then I began the trip north. The weather was again beautiful, but that morning the Weather Channel had showed a storm front around Tampa. Within fifty miles a light rain had started. I continued to ride, hoping it would quit, but I soon stopped under an overpass to put on my rainsuit.

The VS1400 was a great ride for this Florida trip.

With this, a peculiar cycle began. In Florida, thunderstorms commonly start and stop in a matter of minutes, and it seemed that every time I stopped to put on the rainsuit, the rain stopped. Then the suit would get uncomfortable, and I'd stop again to remove it. When I did, the rain began again. I ended up stopping more than I liked and finally decided to just keep the rainsuit on and deal with the discomfort. It became a moot point, however; by the time I reached Tampa, the rain had come to stay. By Gainesville, I'd had enough. I was at the midway point in the return trip, and it was as good a place as any to stop. By that time, all I wanted was a hot shower, dry clothes, and a good meal—in that order.

The next day (Sunday), I decided to make a straight shot back on I-75 so I could get home in time to unwind before the start of the workweek. It was beautiful weather all the way.

All in all, the trip was a good one. The high spots of the week were Highway 98 in the Panhandle, the east coast north of Daytona, the coastal roads on the west coast, and Sanibel and Captiva Islands. Riding the east and west coast north of populated areas and the lesser-known interior roads of Florida is definitely the way to tour the Sunshine State—but maybe not all in one week. I think I would have enjoyed this tour more had I avoided the east coast and ridden down US 27 on the western side of the state, detouring out to some of the small towns on the Gulf. I would also have gotten more out of some of the travel days if I had kept a more leisurely pace, with more stops in areas I hadn't seen before.

A dedicated fisherman at sunrise on an east coast beach north of Daytona

Things I would do differently on the next ride:

- Cover less ground: I rode 2,000 miles in ten days. If I had limited the scope to Destin and the west coast, I would have had more time to relax and absorb the flavor of the area.
- Go in late spring/early fall: Daytime temperatures in the low 80s rather than upper 90s would have been much more comfortable.
- Pack less: I needed a more spartan mind-set when packing, cutting clothing by a third.

I'll tell you this: I will do this more often. When traveling by motorcycle on backcountry roads and highways, you get so much more out of the experience than when traveling by car that there is no comparison. Driving is travel, motorcycling is an adventure. Although I grew up in Florida and had been back many times, on this tour, I feel like I finally got around to seeing some of The Real Florida.

Pine Island, which is very close to Sanibel Island, is a similarly tropical locale.

# THE ROAD GOES ON FOREVER

>>> This travelogue is about a July 2002 trip to the western United States that my wife (then fiancée), Lora, and I took. The trip had all the factors that go into a great motorcycling adventure: grand scenery, challenging roads, a great bike, and new locations. The tour became the subject of a series of two travel articles titled "The Road Goes on Forever," parts 1 and 2, published by *Roadbike* magazine in its August and September 2005 issues. Below is the original story, with updated information in brackets. At the end is a little something extra—a view of the tour from the passenger seat, written by Lora (not previously published).

Left: The Cathedral Group of the Teton Range viewed across Jenny Lake
Above: Yellowstone Lake in the southeastern section of the park

## Utah to Wyoming on the Gold Wing

I have logged many a mile touring the southeastern United States, from Florida to the North Carolina Outer Bank Islands, the Blue Ridge Parkway, and North Georgia. Ever since I got back on a motorcycle, I have dreamed of touring the western United States, but lack of vacation time, funds, or opportunity always seemed to postpone such a trip for another year. In 2002, however, everything fell into place for that dream to come true. The week of the July 4th holiday, I found myself and my fiancée, Lora, on a plane to Salt Lake City, where we had reserved a Honda Gold Wing from the Cruise America corporation for five days of touring the Wild West.

I found the Gold Wing to be a great bike for touring the West.

The plan was to arrive in Salt Lake City on the evening of July 2, pick up the bike the next morning, and return it on July 8. Our choice of direction and distance from Salt Lake would depend on what areas promised the most favorable weather conditions for an enjoyable vacation. Checking the week's weather reports just before our departure, we decided to head north to Yellowstone National Park, then travel into Montana and Idaho.

Weather in Atlanta was typical for summer—hot and humid with a chance for afternoon or evening thunderstorms—and we arrived at the airport to find our 7 p.m. flight delayed for bad weather. En route to the gate, Lora had her shoes checked for explosives three times. (My loafers apparently didn't look nearly as threatening.) Finally, Lora, her suspicious footwear, and I were allowed to board the plane, which took off at about 9:30 p.m. After a three-hour flight, a wait to claim baggage, and what seemed like a long cab ride, we arrived at our hotel well after 11 p.m. Salt Lake time—2 a.m. eastern standard time. Such are the woes of modern-day airline travel.

The next morning we arrived at the Cruise America location on State Street in Salt Lake. We were given a brand new champagne-colored Gold Wing with 4 miles on the odometer. I had test ridden an older model Gold Wing some years ago but hadn't spent any significant time on one before or since. My own motorcycle weighs in at a bit over 500 pounds dry, and I found the transition to a 1,000-plus-pound motorcycle (an 800-pound bike plus rider, passenger, and packed weight) to be a bit of a learning experience for the first few days. Due to the bike's higher center of gravity and greater weight, slow speed maneuvers took some getting used to, but once we were moving faster than 5 miles per hour, the bike was a breeze to handle.

The route we planned to take was US Route 89 North to Wyoming to visit Jackson Hole, Grand Teton, and Yellowstone National Parks for the first two days of our trip. After that, we would travel across the western portion of Montana into Idaho to ride as many of the scenic highways as the remainder of time would allow. Our first day's progress was slowed north of Ogden, Utah, by road construction on Highway 89. What we found was not your typical highway construction. At two different areas south of Bear Lake, the highway was reduced to gravel road for several miles, requiring speeds under 15 miles per hour. This made for a treacherous ride. That I was a novice riding a motorcycle of this size made the experience that much more unnerving.

Fed by the runoff of small glaciers in the surrounding Tetons, Jackson Lake is beautiful but a bit chilly for most swimmers.

Near Alpine, Wyoming, going through a third section of construction road, we were treated to a water truck wetting down the gravel and dirt immediately in front of us, making conditions even worse. At one point, I felt the rear tire lose traction, and for a moment, I thought we would end up in the dirt. Fortunately, we made it through safely, without incident. My advice for those wishing to tour anywhere out here: Check the Internet for the current state of construction work on state highways. Most states have websites that allow you to check road construction status, and this small effort pays big dividends.

[Author's note: I had been riding for six years prior to renting the Gold Wing, and that experience helped me through these incidents while I was getting used to the heavier bike. If you are new or relatively new to riding, you will want to rent a motorcycle that you can confidently handle right now. Leave the bigger bikes you dream of riding for another trip, when you have gained the necessary miles and skills.]

Except for the sections under repair, US 89 is a beautiful road—sweeping curves, with a low-challenge factor and great scenery. The Bear Lake area is a definite highlight, with its ice-blue color, white-sand banks, and surrounding pine forest, which gives the air a subtle pine scent for miles.

We reached Jackson Hole, Wyoming, after seven hours and some 270 miles of riding, arriving about 7:30 p.m. Due to the July 4th holiday, hotel rooms were scarce, but we found one on our second stop. The Red Lion Wyoming Inn is among the more upscale hotels in this well-known resort area, offering first-class service and amenities. You pay a premium price for staying there, but if—as in our case—you've been a bit harried on your first day's adventures, you don't mind a little pampering.

## Grand Teton and Yellowstone

**T**he next morning, we were off for a ride through Grand Teton National Park, then on to Yellowstone National Park. If you have never traveled out here, no amount of description will prepare you for the vastness of scale found everywhere in the open areas of the West. The Appalachians are beautiful, but they don't hold a candle to the impressiveness of the Rockies, which include the Teton Range. The range comprises thirty-seven slate-gray jagged peaks that push straight up from a 5,000-foot plateau to stand out against a deep blue sky. Most of this range is above the tree line and highlighted by permafrost. A dozen peaks rise more than 12,000 feet; the tallest, at 13,700 feet, is Grand Teton, a part of the Cathedral Group of peaks. The side road off Highway 89 up to Jenny Lake is a must-see; the lake works as a massive reflecting pool to enhance the already spectacular view.

Left: Teton's Cathedral Group, with Grand Teton at center
Above: A pause on Hwy 89 North, on our way to Yellowstone

Highway 89 takes you to the south entrance of Yellowstone National Park. Along the way, the change in viewing angle of the Teton Range evolves from perpendicular to almost parallel, with Jenny Lake reflecting the mountains all the way to Yellowstone.

Despite their proximity to each other, the two parks are remarkably different. Whereas the attraction of Grand Teton is its stark features and remote nature, the appeal of Yellowstone is its more intimate feeling. Here, you can enjoy close views of the hot springs and geysers, the lakes and waterfalls, and the wildlife, including deer and elk, moose, bison, and bald eagles. Groups of stopped cars with vacationers pointing and taking photographs are sure signs that some species of park wildlife is congregating near the roadside.

Lora had made reservations for the evening at the Days Inn in the town of West Yellowstone, located just outside the park's west entrance, so the plan for the day was to ride around the southwestern side of the park and take in Old Faithful and the Shoshone Geyser Basin. If time allowed, we would ride across the center of the park to see the Upper

and Lower Falls in the Grand Canyon of the Yellowstone on the northeastern side. (The main roads inside the park are referred to as the Grand Loop and form a figure 8. The center road runs through the center of the 8.) Unfortunately, roadwork inside the park—specifically between Madison Junction and the Norris Junction, the stretch leading up to the center road—reduced the road surface to loose gravel. This would make access by motorcycle to the eastern side of the park another stressful undertaking. Having already had touch-and-go experiences on Highway 89, I wanted to avoid pushing our luck, so we called it a night and checked into the hotel.

[Update: You can check the park's website ahead of time to discover which roads in Yellowstone are under construction and make your sightseeing plans accordingly. You'll find plenty of other planning information there, as well (see www.nps.gov/yell/).]

The next morning, we decided on an ambitious riding day, traveling back around the southern end of the park to take a circular 110-mile ride to the north entrance, thereby avoiding the road construction. The drawback to this change was that we would be exiting the park on the north end, rather than the west as planned, which meant it would take us longer to reach the roads in Idaho we wanted to explore later in the week.

Planned stops for the day included Yellowstone Lake, the Upper and Lower Falls at Artist's Point, Tower Junction, and Mammoth Hot Springs. The differing topography—from borderline desert with hot springs and volcanic geysers, to the immense Yellowstone Lake, to the waterfalls and mountainous areas—was

Left: A moose gets a drink from the Yellowstone River. Right: Viewing the Lower Falls at Artist's Point, you can understand how the location received its name.

Crested Pool as viewed from the Geyser Hill Loop Trail at the Upper Geyser Basin

spectacular and kept our interest the entire way, but this was not a quick ride. With stops to view the sites and get food and fuel and slowdowns for all the RVs traveling the roads, the tour took the entire day.

We arrived at our last stop, Mammoth Hot Springs, at about 4:30 on Friday afternoon. The last time I was here, in 1978, I thought this area was one of the most spectacular in the park, with many active springs belching steam and water, and an amazing array of colorful algae. Twenty-plus years later, a number of those springs had gone dormant, dried to a powder white, so when I saw the area again, I considered it less impressive. Despite the inactivity, the springs are still an interesting feature of the park. [Author's note: According to the park rangers, the springs change over time, with old ones drying up and new ones coming into existence. Yet the overall volume of water discharged remains about the same. So don't be surprised if the area looks much different from one visit to the next.]

Since our arrival, the weather had been sauna-like hot, near 100 degrees, and very dry; overnight

A deer atop Minerva Terrace limestone formation.

temperatures never dropped below the mid-seventies. The old joke is "yeah, but it's a dry heat," and that was absolutely true. Here, you did not sweat—you baked. The heat took its toll on our energy reserves, and lots of water and a good sun-block were absolute necessities. Walking the Mammoth Springs area added to the cooked, put-a-fork-in-it, feeling for Lora and me.

Above: Palette Spring formation, 1978. Overleaf: Silex Spring near Old Faithful.

# Montana

From Yellowstone's north entrance, there are no roads leading west; traveling north is the only option. We spent the rest of the afternoon riding up a mostly arrow-straight, hot, and dry US 89 at a crisp 75 miles per hour (the speed limit in much of Montana). We arrived at Livingston, where we could pick up I-90, and got a room at the Best Western.

Saturday morning we were off again, heading west on I-90. We were now past the halfway point in our five days of travel, and there was still so much to see. I had gotten fairly well used to the extra heft of the Gold Wing, but handling the large bike put an added drain on my batteries. Being on a bike all day in these conditions definitely wears down both operator and passenger. Yet I wouldn't have missed this for the world. The roads and surrounding scenery out here are incredible. You can ride all day heading straight toward mountains in the distance, and they never seem to get any closer. Plains between mountain foothills seemingly cover half the state, and the road you're on is the only sign of civilization as far as the eye can see. Every once in a while, you ride through a very small town with few signs of human habitation. And when I say very small, out here,

Hwy 287, near Three Forks, Montana

I mean it—a crossroad with one gas station, one diner, and one hardware store. You are traveling in some sparsely populated country here, with fuel available only in widely separated towns. The Gold Wing carries about 5 gallons and has about a 200-mile range, so we were never worried. If you decide to tour out here on a bike with a smaller tank, fill up whenever you can.

Using the cruise-control feature on the Gold Wing is a necessity. I found the handgrips to be a bit on the smallish size, causing my hands to cramp after a while. A day of riding this road without cruise control would surely have resulted in a case of claw hand. Any concerns you might have about setting the cruise at 75-plus miles per hour disappears out here.

Lora and the Gold Wing after we stopped to don our rain gear on US 93, a beautiful road to travel. This is one not to miss if you tour this part of the country.

If you counted on both hands the number of cars and trucks going by in the opposite direction all day, you would still have a digit or two unused by nightfall. Any large animal roaming the plains could be seen and allowed for long before you reached it. Out here, you cover the miles, basking in the wide-open spaces.

The route through Montana had been convoluted, hastily reworked due to our unplanned northern exit from Yellowstone. After exiting I-90 at Three Forks, we took US Route 287 South. Although the map legend doesn't indicate that 287 is a scenic highway, there aren't any losers out here as far as the roads go. Long sweeping curves and gently rolling hills surrounded by mountain foothills are the norm. Highway 287 cuts a right turn at Ennis, taking us due west. It connects with Montana 41 to MT 278 then MT 43 past I-15, later ending at Highway 93 just over the Idaho border.

# Idaho

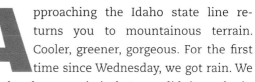

pproaching the Idaho state line returns you to mountainous terrain. Cooler, greener, gorgeous. For the first time since Wednesday, we got rain. We stopped to don our rain jackets; we didn't need rain pants thanks to the coverage of the Wing's large fairing. The big tourer's fairing is designed for looking through the windshield, not over it. I'm not crazy about looking through motorcycle windshields; although in dry weather, I didn't notice any optical distortion from the shield and got used to it. Had this been my motorcycle, I would have treated the windshield with a wetting agent to allow raindrops to blow off. Without it, seeing through the windshield in the rain was impossible. Until the rain ended and I could dry the windshield, I had to sit

with a stiff back to allow a line of sight over it (being of shorter stature). The Wing's windshield has about 4 inches of upward adjustment, so again if it had been my bike, I would have it shortened it to allow a clear line of sight over it in rainy weather and adjusted it up for more wind protection in dry.

US 93 in Idaho is one beautiful stretch of road and a must-ride if you are traveling out here. For all of its 107 miles from the state line to Idaho 75, the highway meanders along, following the gentle curves of the Salmon River. The foothills and the river that run on either side of this road make for some spectacular unspoiled scenery. Other than the few quaint western towns that it runs through, Highway 93 is totally unpopulated and offers excellent scenic views every mile of the ride.

The late afternoon was upon us. At a stop for gas in Challis, I asked the girl behind the counter about places to stop for the night. I explained that we were heading up toward Idaho 21, and she suggested staying in Stanley, assuring me that there were plenty of hotels and finding a room would not be a problem. On ID 75, we headed west toward Stanley, as did the Salmon River, as pretty and picturesque as before.

One of the best experiences of our visit to Stanley was this stunning sunset.

## Mountain Adventure in the Dark

Upon our arrival in Stanley, we were shocked to find out that there were no vacancies in any hotel. What I had been led to believe was a well-established resort location was actually more of a small hamlet with three hotels. Very pretty, very quaint, very picturesque . . . and very small. [Update: Stanley does have more lodging options now. If only the town had started building them a few years sooner.]

With a sinking feeling in my stomach—and in Lora's too, no doubt—we stopped at the last hotel in town, flashing its no vacancy sign, and asked about accommodations elsewhere in the area. Nothing doing. Our best chance at finding a place to stay for the night, we were told, was at least 60 miles away.

The rain was just ending and nightfall was approaching. We were tired and way past the point at which we should be traveling. It was the July 4th weekend, and I should have realized that lots of tourists would have the same idea we had. I had my cell phone with me, and Lora had brought a AAA guide with her, which listed virtually every hotel and motel in the state. It would have been simple to call ahead earlier in the day to check, but I didn't think to do it. A little forethought would have kept this from happening. A hard lesson to learn at that point.

Sun Valley, Ketchum, and Boise were our closest options; the first two were about 60 miles away, and the last one was about 110 miles away. On the map, both Sun Valley and Ketchum appeared to be small towns. Not wanting to be caught in the same situation, we opted to ride to Boise.

As we rode south on 21 toward Boise, the sun made its exit for the day and the last remnants of daylight began rapidly fading. Idaho 21 is a well-known road in this area and one I came here to ride, but not like this. I knew that on the way down the mountain, we would encounter a dangerous combination of circumstances—a dark, unlit, very twisty mountain road, the possibility of large wild animals around any curve, and an already long day in the

At one point we were treated to a double rainbow arcing over the mountains to the south—another in dozens of excellent photo ops.

We had been on the road since 10:30 a.m., and it was now 9:30 p.m. Because Idaho is so far north and it was midsummer, the sun was still visible in the sky, and it would be at least thirty minutes before it would sink below the mountain. But with eleven hours in the saddle, we wanted to call it a day. Unfortunately, we would soon find out that we would be on the road a bit longer.

saddle. In these conditions, the 110-mile ride would take much longer than it would have in daylight. Still, there was nothing to do but buck up and get it over as quickly and as safely as possible. I know Lora was aware of the dangers we were facing, and we would be vigilantly watching the road all the way down the mountain for the next three-plus hours. At least the rain had stopped, and the sky was clear.

The road was about as we expected. Although we were lucky not to have any deer or elk jump out in front of us on the ride down, there were several of them just off the road on most curves and close to the roads on the pullouts and road shoulders. Kudos to the Gold Wing here—the bright lights lit up the road very well (a pair of reflecting fauna eyes in the darkness is an unnerving thing!), and using the horn, which is louder than many car horns, we scared encountered animals farther away from the road.

Immediately inside the Boise city limits, we stopped at the very first hotel that we found, which

was a Best Western. It was 12:30 a.m., and we had been on the motorcycle for an exhausting fourteen hours. Thankfully, rooms were available, but looking as we probably did at that moment, I don't think the clerk would have had the heart to turn us away in any case.

Lora appeared beyond exhausted as she walked into the hotel with tired eyes and a glazed expression on her face. I thought she was going to hate me forever. I wouldn't have blamed her.

## Back up the Mountain

The morning brought more beautiful weather and, at least for me, a renewed sense of adventure. After the previous night, I didn't want to jump enthusiastically into a discussion of the day's activities, fearing a less than equal response on Lora's part. We hadn't talked about a riding destination, or even if there was one, but not wanting the trip to end on a bad note, I was hoping to make the last day a good one. While Lora got up and going, I took the bike to a local drive-in car wash to clean it up. The previous four days had put quite a coat of grime on it, and I hate riding a dirty motorcycle. Boise in the daytime is a beautiful town: very clean, very well kept, and with the mountains as a backdrop, very Pacific Northwest. At the car wash, I struck up a conversation with a local resident. I mentioned what a beautiful area it was, and he said "Yeah, we know. Don't tell anybody."

Back at the room, I consulted the map to see if there were any scenic destinations close by that we could ride for the day before heading back to Utah in the morning. The best choice was SR 21, the road we had come down the previous evening.

Obviously, any enjoyment of the road—of the ride or the scenery—had been lost in the darkness, so I didn't feel like we'd seen it. I did not, however, look forward to making this suggestion to Lora. To her credit, she didn't throw her riding boots at me when I did, and although not entirely enthusiastic, she said she would keep an open mind. A Perkins restaurant was within a stone's throw of the hotel, so we walked over for breakfast.

Fortunately for me, we got into a conversation with a very friendly waitress, telling her about our tour and the previous evening's ordeal. The waitress said that we really should see Idaho 21 in the daytime, as it was a gorgeous road and well worth the ride. This was apparently enough to win Lora

This stretch of Idaho 21 from Boise to Stanley is called the Ponderosa Pine Scenic Byway, a fact we appreciated much more in the daylight.

Highway 75 carried us past pine trees and a flowing river in meandering curves rather than twisty ones, a nice change for the day.

over, and soon we were heading into the mountains once again.

After all is said and done, I am glad we didn't miss this. Idaho 21 is another real winner of a road, and the ride up bore little resemblance to the white-knuckled one down the previous evening. There's more of the incredible Idaho scenery that we'd come to know and love, along with enough "twisties" to keep it interesting.

Once again, the Gold Wing was a dream to handle; it's quite surprising to me that a motorcycle of this size handles so nimbly. Even fully loaded, the Gold Wing is a confidence-inspiring machine on a road like this; I never felt like its size was an impediment on the curves. You just lean her over, and she tucks in and throttles right out effortlessly.

We rode through Stanley and headed south on Idaho 75 once again. While this section of road is not as challenging a ride as the section we rode the previous day, it is nonetheless as beautiful in its own way as any in the area. Here, the curves are

more sweeping and less twisty, and on the ride up to Galena Summit at 8,700 feet, you can stop and view the valley behind and ID 75 as they stretch out below. Farther south, we took a break in Sun Valley, where we found the only Starbuck's Coffee in 1,500-plus miles of riding over the past five days. Ah, civilization. A mocha cappuccino for her, a regular coffee for me, a shared scone, and we were rolling again. At Bellevue, we headed south toward Interstate 84, and the heat of the day reached its peak. The mercury hit 101 degrees, desert dry. Even at 75 miles per hour, the rushing air didn't provide much relief. As we moved into farmland, huge watering machines feeding crops raised the humidity to the point that it felt like we were riding through a steam bath perfumed by manure. Very pleasant.

Near Twin Falls, it was back on the interstate for the ride to Pocatello, where we decided to spend the last evening before our return to Salt Lake City. Not accustomed to packing for motorcycle travel, Lora had brought a pair of high-heeled sandals with her

Galena Summit forms part of the Sawtooth Scenic Byway. The ride to the 8,700-foot summit is worth the effort because you can get a great view of the valley.

on this trip, and they were the source of many a joke at her expense during the previous week. "Not much call for high-heeled sandals out here, ma'am." She took the opportunity to wear them to dinner, so as not to call packing them a total loss.

## Vacation's End

I n the morning, we started back to Salt Lake City to turn the bike in and get to the airport for the flight home. The ride south on I-15 was as it had been every other place this week—hot. Just south of Ogden, at a section of stop-and-go traffic on the interstate (road construction), the Wing began to overheat and the engine temperature needle climbed until it pinged the red zone. I thought I would have to park the bike and shut it down, but luckily traffic got moving and the engine cooled to normal operating temperature. It was the only time the Gold Wing gave me any cause for concern, and I have since read reports on the occasional overheating problem of some earlier models of the 1800 Gold

Wing. [Update: It is my understanding that the Gold Wing overheating problem was addressed in a recall with replacement of engine control modules and, in some cases, the engine temperature gauge in 2001 to 2003 Gold Wings. Later models incorporated larger radiators and fans to correct the problem.]

We turned the bike back in to Cruise America at 1:30 p.m., having racked up 1,847 miles for the five-day trip, about a 308-mile daily average. The folks at Cruise America were great, and we were checked in efficiently and quickly, just as we had been when we checked the bike out five days earlier. The bike was a joy—in excellent condition and ready to roll—and the rental experience was problem free.

As for the week, no description can suffice. If you have not traveled out here, prepare yourself for a life-changing experience. The United States is one of the most naturally beautiful countries in the world, and areas such as these in the West must be seen to be believed. Get on the bike—there are lots of miles to cover.

Here I am, standing in Grand Teton National Park. I had a slightly different view of our trip out west, from the backseat of the Gold Wing.

## Backseat Diary: Lora C. Riley

**D**ay 1, July 3. We picked up the rented bike at Cruise America—a brand-new Honda Gold Wing with 4 miles on the odometer! We had both overpacked, and several items had to be left at the hotel front desk to be picked up on our return. (Lesson learned: pack light, do laundry on the road, and leave the black high-heeled sandals at home.) Loading the remainder on the bike was a bit of a chore, but as soon as we loaded up, our adventure got under way. Being the experienced rider that he is, Phil quickly adapted to the handling of the fully loaded Gold Wing, which weighed considerably more than his motorcycle.

Going north on US Route 89 out of Salt Lake City, we crossed through the southeast corner of Idaho, and passed through the scenic Bear Lake area. The blue-green of the lake against the mountainous background was absolutely spectacular, and the smell of pine filled the air. Continuing on 89 North into Wyoming through the Bridger National Forest, we followed the scenic route along the Snake River. The road elevation increased as we continued the ride, with a shear drop-off to the Snake River below. It was here that we unexpectedly encountered a loose gravel roadway. Unknown to us, portions of Highway 89 were under construction, reduced at times to dirt and gravel. As if that weren't bad enough, through one section of the construction, a water truck was wetting down the dirt road, as well. Needless to say, it was white-knuckle time for a couple of miles as we passed through this construction site.

**Day 2, July 4**. After the first long day of riding, I quickly learned to have water on hand to prevent dehydration, moisturizer for my lips and the corners of my eyes, and plenty of sunscreen. Continuing on 89 North, we made our way through the snowcapped mountains of the Tetons, stopping along the way to photograph "God's Country." Words can't describe how beautiful this place is, and I am not sure that even a photo from a highly skilled artist could portray the deep contrasting colors that seemed to touch our souls. Once we entered Yellowstone National Park, our first mission of the day was to see Old Faithful. We spent hours touring the geyser basin, where multicolored algae grew in near-boiling water and the area often seemed to resemble an alien landscape. It was also our first encounter with the wildlife—elk so close that you could touch them, along with a magnificent bald eagle feeding chicks in its nest.

**Day 3, July 5**. Due to roadway construction through the center of the park, we decided to take the long way around, and I am glad that we did. Stopping at Yellowstone's Upper and Lower Falls and the Sulphur Cauldron, we encountered several bison grazing in a field across the road. The bison were not at all intimidated by our presence, and

A bison in Yellowstone Park that Phil got a little too close to in his enthusiasm to get the right photographic shot.

one large bull menacingly stared Phil down when he got too close while shooting photographs.

We departed the park through the North Gate on Highway 89 into Montana. I can understand why they call this part of Montana Big Sky Country. Never-ending green pastures are set against mountains covered in pine and white birch trees, and the sky is a crystal blue with white, puffy clouds that seem to go up to infinity.

**Day 4, July 6**. The day began gray and overcast, with storm clouds on the horizon. As we crossed over into Idaho, a storm front moved in and the wind began to kick up. Great gusts hit us hard and without warning, and one nearly took my head off. Not stopping to put on our rain gear and then failing to outrun the summer squall, we received a good soaking. Once out of the storm, however, our clothing dried quickly in the unusually high temperatures and extremely low humidity.

We continued south on the scenic route of Highway 93 as it ran the length of the Salmon River. What a fantastically beautiful ride traveling along the base of the mountains on one side and the river on the other. The earthy, slightly sweet pine smell in the air could have been bottled with a label reading "Nature at Its Finest." Later, on Idaho 75, another summer squall hit us, but we were prepared this time, having stopped to don our rain gear at the sight of storm clouds moving in. After riding just a few miles in the light rain, we saw it—a double rainbow stretching high across the sky! We had to get a photo of this. While Phil was capturing this awesome moment, the rain turned to pea-size hail. (What next? Snow?)

Proceeding to Stanley, we found a quaint little town with three small hotels . . . and no vacancies. (Important lesson: on a holiday `weekend [July 4th], it pays to call ahead and make reservations.) Choosing what we considered the best option, we continued on toward Boise, another 110 miles, with the last of the light fading. Stopping at a small campground, we changed out of our wet clothing and prepared for the cold ride in the dark. Then Phil explained to me what I already knew but didn't want to hear: that wildlife; dark, winding, mountainous roads; and motorcycles are not a good combination. So I held on tightly to the grab bars and prepared for the ride of my life. Riding pitch-black mountain roads with switchbacks, diminishing radius turns, and wildlife on almost every pullout, we pressed onward through the Boise National Forest. Cold and scared to death, with my eyes frozen on the roadway ahead, I knew that if it hadn't been for Phil's years of riding experience, this venture might have been a disaster. Three and a half hours later, at 12:30 a.m., we reached Boise. Our agreement was that we would stop at the first hotel that we laid our exhausted eyeballs on, and we did. It was another Best Western at the Boise City limits. We had been on the motorcycle for fourteen hours.

Above: Here I am in my rain gear beside US 93. This time we got our gear out at the first sign of dark clouds. Right: The Lower Falls River in Yellowstone Park

Double rainbow on Idaho 75, one of the many moments to treasure from our trip

Idaho 21, snapped from the backseat, as we wound our way up the mountain

Day 5, July 7. Phil was concerned that we might not be on speaking terms, but I reassured him. He then cautiously approached the subject of the day's activities. The road that we traveled in the dark the prior evening was reportedly one of the most spectacular rides in this entire area, and Phil wanted to see it in the daylight. (Now may

Items with a southwestern motif are displayed at a Sun Valley store.

to work, and as a result, I believe that we got some very interesting photographic opportunities that we might otherwise have missed out on.

**Day 6, July 8**. The ride from Pocatello, Idaho, where we'd stopped for the night, to Salt Lake City, Utah, was relatively uneventful, with the exception of a grasshopper flying into Phil's helmet, which added some humor to the day's ride. We arrived back at Cruise America, where our adventure had started five days earlier. From the passenger's point of view, the Gold Wing was a superb choice for the tour. It was smooth as silk, with little or no vibration, as well as sure-footed on the twisting mountains, and it offered extremely comfortable passenger accommodations.

With 1,800-plus miles on the bike now behind us, I would have expected my backside to be numb, but that wasn't the case at all. Having traveled on motorcycles as operator and passenger, I can tell you that with the right operator and bike, the experience from the backseat can be just as spectacular and rewarding as that from the front—and just as comfortable.

be a good time to explain that I don't handle heights very well, especially on a two-wheeled vehicle.) Reluctantly, I gave in. Phil, sensing that he was pushing the envelope regarding my stress level, played a little psychological trick on me by handing me the camera. My mission, should I decide to accept it, was to capture the switchbacks and other scenery worth noting from the backseat. The trick seemed

# THE ROAD BACK

>>> Two thousand six marked my fiftieth year on the planet. Time for reflection, refraction, definitely taking stock and maybe buying stock. I'd been through a few midlife changes. I'd gotten married and left my career in engineering to give writing and photography a full-time shot. While the income is down, happiness is up.

I took this tour in June of that year, from Atlanta to Charleston, for a reunion with friends from my air force days. They are among the best people I know, and I am fortunate to still have them with me on life's journey. I dedicate this travelogue to them.

The piece, edited for space, was first published as "Favorite Ride" by *Rider* in December 2006. Here's the unabridged story.

Left: New and old-style transportation in Battery Park, Charleston
Above: A discrete entryway to one of Charleston's many art galleries

# Coming of Age

Thirty years ago, in 1976, I was in the US Air Force, stationed in Charleston, South Carolina. I had gotten there the previous year and spent the majority of my four-year enlistment there. In the seventies, the Charleston area was not quite the lovely spot it is today. The area around the Charleston military base was a somewhat depressing combination of used-car lots selling mostly rundown transportation and dive bars, commonly referred to as "clip joints," that catered mostly to military personnel. When you combine the lack of entertainment with a $300-a-month airman's paycheck and the energy of a twenty-year-old, you get a pretty frustrated young person.

The saving grace in my life was the group of friends I fell in with that year. It was a crowd of eight or so, and we became an ensemble cast of characters for the next couple of years, until my enlistment ended in 1978. Their good natures, senses of fun, and senses of humor made my air force service time in Charleston one of the best times of my life. As inevitably happens with those in the military, assignments send some to new locations, enlistments end, and friends go their separate ways.

Over the years, however, I maintained regular contact with two of this group, Bob Maahs and Liz Belk, and I saw each of them from time to time. These two managed to keep in contact with

Five of my coming-of-age US Air Force buddies and me back in 1976. Top row, left to right: Bob Lowell, Liz Belk, Mary (Maahs) Parker. Bottom row, left to right: Lezlie (Sturgis) Downes, me, Bob Maahs.

This is the updated version of the Windjammer beach bar, where my friends and I hung out in the late seventies. Many good memories!

others, so I knew all were still around. Many times, Bob and I had spoken about organizing a reunion of the group, and (due primarily to his efforts) exactly thirty years later to the summer we had met, we would gather in Charleston once again. For me, the reunion would also be an opportunity for a motorcycle tour, riding the scenic highways in an area where I had lived decades before. Back then, one of the few sources of entertainment was a Sunday drive on the roads and highways northwest of the base. I looked forward to riding those roads again.

The group would meet on Thursday, June 1, and stay through the fourth. Bob had booked rooms at the Holiday Inn in Isle of Palms for the weekend, just 100 yards up the street from a beach bar called the Windjammer, a group hangout back in '76. My wife, Lora, would drive her car, with all necessities for the weekend, and take the interstates to Charleston. I would be free to travel the scenic route. One of the many advantages of having a spouse, I am learning, is that she can pilot the "chase vehicle."

## On the Road Back

Interstate 20 runs due east to Augusta, Georgia, making it the most logical route for the first leg of the trip. At Augusta, Lora would continue on Interstate 20 to Columbia and pick up I-26 into Charleston, while I would head east on rural roads through South Carolina.

Interstate travel on a motorcycle is what it always is—boring and noisy with wind but usually the fastest route between two points. For my fiftieth birthday several months before, my wife had bought me a portable music player, and I had spent the previous two days loading almost every CD in my music collection on it—everything from 1960s and '70s rock to jazz, classical, and new country. The unit is an amazing piece of technology, with a capacity to store more than 1,000 songs on it while fitting neatly in a top pocket. The unit plays on earplug headphones under the helmet, and the BMW's electrically adjustable windshield in its full up position helped to keep wind noise at bay.

My bike presents a great contrast to the 1950s cars in a Hwy 78 junkyard.

Like most music devices of this type, mine has a mode for playing stored music in random order. I thought it might be interesting to let the unit pick the sound track for this trip, which would also eliminate the distraction of pressing buttons while riding. After all, the songs were my choices, and my own favorite music selections—no hunting for radio stations necessary.

We left the house together at 9:30 a.m. I anticipated a six- to seven-hour ride, with stops for photographs along the way. At Augusta I waved to my wife and exited at I-520 East, a loop highway around Augusta, to take State Route 28 East a few miles to US Route 278 for the first leg of the open-country ride. I had picked a route that ran due east: US Route 278 to US Route 78, which would lead to US Route 61 as I approached Charleston. I especially anticipated riding Highway 61, as I remembered it as a particularly beautiful stretch of road. This highway into the Charleston area was a favorite cruising road back then. Many sections featured overhanging trees, dangling Spanish moss, and old southern plantations, such as Middleton Place and Magnolia Gardens, that were converted to state parks.

Once on US 278, I was treated to an open two-lane highway on a bright and sunny day. As it was an early Thursday afternoon in a rural area, traffic was very light, making an interstate speed-limit pace the norm. While it was the beginning of the summer season, temperatures had been cooler than usual—in the mid-eighties with low humidity—so the ride was also very comfortable.

On days like this, it is difficult for me to understand why anyone would be on an interstate. The only advantage I can see is that you're less likely to make a wrong turn. For me, planned route changes are like milestones on the trip, and looking for them is part of the fun. Taking rural roads certainly lessens the monotony of the travel and almost always offers more in the way of varying scenery and interesting sights, including the unusual, as well as lower traffic levels. In this particular case, the rural route to Charleston is also more direct than the interstate, so although towns occasionally slow the pace, the shorter distance makes travel time approximately equal. When I'm on the motorcycle, rural highways are the only way to travel.

West of Williston, a short connecting road (SR 781) linked 278 to Highway 78, for the next leg east. As had been the case all day, the roads were clear, the weather cool, and the ride enjoyable. Near the Williston-Elko area, I came across an old car junkyard that featured primarily vintage 1950s vehicles. I have always loved these cars, and I owned a '57 Ford sedan in the early '90s. I stopped and got some great photographs, juxtaposing the modern motorcycle with the anachronistic and now thoroughly rusting examples of classic Americana. Sad in a way. Cars such as these have such style; it's unfortunate to find them simply wasting away in a field, unappreciated. It was good to see the large group of them parked together, though. If you have to grow old, it's good to grow old with friends.

Farther east, I rode onto Highway 61. The skies began to cloud up, readying for summer's typical afternoon rain. I debated whether to stop to don my rainsuit, but the roads were wet, indicating that the rain had already passed through the area. Several

US Route 61 offers a quiet canopy of overhanging trees and Spanish moss.

On a foggy day in 1976, I captured this shot of the pier at the Isle of Palms. The pier was later blown away by Hurricane Hugo in 1989.

miles ahead I could see open sky and sunshine, so I kept riding. I did ride through some light rain, but the windshield and forward movement kept me mostly dry. The cloudy sky and light rain cooled the day and the ride nicely, but the pavement was wet and the older road a little uneven, so I slowed down to avoid small indentations that held puddles of water.

North of Summerville, the rain stopped, but the skies remained partially overcast and the area cool. This section of 61 comprises some of the best parts of the road, and I was very glad to see that it hadn't changed much in thirty years. Great old oaks with hanging Spanish moss still line the road in several sections, giving you the feeling of riding through a large, organic tunnel. This is one beautiful ride. The Ashley River separates this area from Charleston proper, and there are few bridges and roads connecting it to the city. I suspect that is why this highway has remained mostly unchanged. Closer to Charleston, housing communities and retail establishments have sprung up on the western side of the highway.

I-526, the elevated loop built in this city in the past twenty years, definitely helps move traffic through and around Charleston, and it is only one of the improvements in the roads here. Thirty years ago, Highway 17 was the major north-south path through the city, and the road was old even then

and had not been improved in some time. I-26 from Columbia was the only interstate that made it to Charleston, and it came in from the west and did not go through the city. Back then, it was a difficult town to get around in, with only local rural roads and highways allowing access to either the Isle of Palms beach to the north or Folly Beach to the south.

Today I-526 connects both areas and loops around Charleston, making the transition around the city quick and easy. Kudos to the city. I hopped on the loop and got over to the Isle of Palms area in ten minutes. The road takes you past the Port of Charleston, and the elevated view really gives you a perspective on how big port operations are here. The cargo ships, stacked crates and containers of goods, and cranes to load and off-load are massive and take up the entire Cooper River to the left and right sides of the interstate for what seems like a mile out.

Exiting I-526 to US 17 on the north end of town landed me at Mount Pleasant. A few miles north, US 17 led to US 517 East, which is another of the newer roads in the Charleston area. A nice, scenic, well-built highway, 517 led directly into Isle of Palms, going over undeveloped marshland on the way. Crossing State Route 703 into the beach area and taking a quick right turn at Ocean Boulevard got me to the hotel.

# Reunion

I arrived in time to meet some of the group checking in at the hotel. Bob Maahs and his wife, Nancy, had come down from Virginia with another member of the group, Mike Kondas, and his wife, Judy. I hadn't seen Mike in thirty years. We all instantly reconnected and agreed to meet for a drink at the 'Jammer down the street after getting settled. Others of the group would be coming in on Friday. I parked, locked, and covered the bike, and headed to the room. Lora had already checked in.

Friday afternoon, the last of the group arrived and joined us on the beach. Liz Belk brought her two lovely daughters, Linsey and Sierra, and Bob Lowell from Boston brought son Brendan. I thought it interesting that Liz's oldest daughter and Bob's son, both in their early twenties, were about the same age that many of us had been when we were stationed here. The last two arrivals were Bill "Tree" Ammons, given that nickname because of his

height of 6 feet 9 inches, and Bill Waters, who was a neighbor at the duplex apartment rented by several of us back then. As most of us lived on base at the time, the apartment was considered party central by the group and was a daily gathering place. Tree stayed in Charleston after being discharged from the air force and had a twenty-five-plus-year career with Bell South. As he was now a Charleston native, we appointed him our tour guide.

We all spent the day on the beach, catching up, consuming low to moderate amounts of alcohol, laughing, and getting sunburned. Friday night, Tree steered the group to a great restaurant called The Boathouse for dinner, and afterward we returned to the Windjammer to hang for the night.

Back in the 1970s on the Isle of Palms, the Windjammer had been one of the few thriving businesses on this beach. It was a laid-back beach bar close to an area that was mostly residential, with little else around it. The Windjammer had wooden steps going

Tree and I, standing side by side, as the group of air force friends enjoy beach time with each other and our families.

Taking in the sand-sculpture contest on Saturday morning was a fun and interesting way to start the day.

We enjoyed a great dinner at The Boathouse Restaurant, thanks to Tree.

in, open doors, and sand directly out the back door, and wood-slat floors. The closest major structure around it was the Isle of Palms fishing pier, a few hundred yards up the beach. When Hurricane Hugo hit the area in the 1989, all of this was blown away, and the newer, trendier, upscale Isle of Palms grew out of the wreckage.

The old, sandy beach bar was gone, but the feel of the new place was still beach bar. It had an excellent

band, the crowd was loose and up on the floor, and the evening was just plain fun. One of the best things about the weekend was that, although it had been thirty years, we all fell in together as if no time had passed. These were still the easiest people I knew to be with, and I think the reason is that we spent our coming-of-age time with each other. We became adults together. It was the first time that most of us had lived on our own, away from family, making our own way in the world. This is the formative group of people who were with me when the real transition from dependent child to independent adult took place. They were there to see me through all that, and I feel as comfortable with them as I do with family.

From conversations that evening, I believe that everyone saw it the same way. Plus, they are just good people: decent, friendly, intelligent. They raised good kids, stuck with and made successful careers, marriages, and lives. I respect their accomplishments. They're salt-of-the-earth people.

We were all a bit older, however. When we were younger, the party might have carried on until much later, but Lora and I peeled off and headed to our room around 1 a.m., and the rest of the group left a short while later. We are not the hard-core partiers that we used to be—thankfully, I think.

The remainder of the weekend was much the same—good company, great fun. Saturday, a sand-sculpture contest took place on the beach, and we all checked that out and then relaxed on the shore for a while. That afternoon, we met at the Windjammer to re-create/update a group photograph that I had taken here in 1976. Ever since we'd begun discussing a reunion, I had wanted to get everyone together to do an updated version of that photograph.

In early evening, following a walking tour of historic downtown Charleston and dinner at Hyman's Seafood on Meeting Street, we all met back at the hotel to laugh over a photo album from our air force days that Liz had brought. A few people had early flights on Sunday, so we said good-bye to them. Those leaving later in the day would meet for breakfast.

After a great breakfast at a place called the Acme Cantina, we all agreed to do this again. Mike commented that he felt more comfortable with this group even after thirty years than he did with most of the people he knew. I offered up my "coming-of-age group" theory; Mike agreed.

An updating of our 1976 photo. Top, left to right: Liz Belk, Mike Kondas, Bob Lowell, Linsey Devenow (Liz's oldest daughter), Bill "Tree" Ammons, Bob Maahs, Bill Waters. Bottom, left to right: Sierra Royster (Liz's youngest daughter), Lora (my wife), me, Judy Kondas, Nancy Maahs (Bob's wife).

# The Road Home

It was time to ride again. One of the great things about taking a vacation on the motorcycle is that the vacation lasts until you reach the front door. When traveling by car or plane, the last day of a vacation often feels like you're simply getting home to return to a routine, with the travel more of a chore than a vacation day. On the bike, there's always the feeling of adventure, coming or going. Going home is not anticlimactic; it's just another interesting day.

Lora had left earlier in the day to travel the interstate route home. I would be stopping periodically for photographs on the way, in the Isle of Palms and in downtown Charleston, and wherever else a good picture presented itself, before heading back toward Augusta and then Atlanta on the same route I had ridden here. Highway 61 was the nicest road west, and worth another ride.

After stops for Isle of Palms seascape photos, pictures of boats on Shem Creek (I take these photos every time I'm here), and the bike in the Charleston Battery area, I returned to and started north on Highway 61. Now, as I settled into travel mode, riding on the highway along the Ashley River (a road driven for recreation back then), the experience took on a flashback quality.

On the previous Tuesday and Wednesday, while loading CDs, I had chosen one by the classic rock band Yes, titled *Close to the Edge*. I put it on the player more as part of the process of loading music than because I expected to listen to it all that much. It was the kind of music I listened to a lot back in the 1970s, but not anything I had paid much attention to in over twenty years. As I heard the familiar opening strains of the twenty-minute-long title track, it seemed that the "ghost in the machine"

Left: Downtown Charleston walkway. Above: A house in Battery Park, Charleston. Overleaf: Shem Creek.

I stopped near Barnwell, on Highway 78, another peaceful spot by the water.

had made a selection that instantly transported me back to that time. Even after not listening to this music regularly since the mid-seventies, I found I still knew every subtle nuance of the music, and could still sing along with the lyrics.

I just smiled and rolled through the curves of the road, taking in the entire déjà vu experience. I just love when things like this happen. It makes me sure that there's more to seemingly random occurrences than chance. If I had been choosing the music myself, I know I would not have picked this song to listen to, but it seemed the perfect choice, causing me to reflect on who I was then and who I am now and to relive a bit of my own history.

When you listen to music while riding, the music takes on elements of a motion picture sound track, as it becomes rolled up in the immediacy of riding the bike—the Zen-like, moment-to-moment attention that must be paid to the task, if you will—

imparting a mood or a flavor that sets the tempo of the ride and of the day. I found myself wishing others could know this experience. This is why I choose riding the motorcycle over other forms of transportation. It is the only mode of travel in which you are driven to be completely in the moment, not always thinking about making time or getting to the destination but simply enjoying where you are and what you're doing. There's an improvisational nature about it, being in the environment and part of it, part of the universe, whatever. How do I describe it without sounding 1960s hippie? It's difficult. At times like this, you are just zooming.

The song ended as I rode out of the most picturesque part of the highway—the route I had traveled the most thirty years ago. Perfect timing. Continuing on, I stopped at Gihvan's Ferry State Park, another favorite spot back then. As it had been most of the weekend, the weather was more than

few exposures on a roll of film, so I pulled off the road for the final pictures of the bike and the highway. While I was stopped, another motorcyclist saw me on the side of the road, slowed, and put on his turn signal, prepared to render assistance. I gave him the OK sign and said thanks, and he waved and rode on. That's just what riders do.

At Augusta, I got back on the interstate, locked the throttle, and made time. Near Covington, the skies clouded over for the daily afternoon rain, and just like it was planned, the music box played The Who's "Love, Reign O'er Me"—again, the appropriate sound track. As had been the case all weekend, I found myself in a light drizzle but rode out of it.

With stops for photos, it had been a long riding day. I totaled about 330 miles from Charleston to Atlanta and pulled into my driveway at around 7:30 p.m. The combination of the one-of-a-kind riding experience with the opportunity to reconnect with great friends made it truly one of the best weekends

Gihvan's Ferry State Park, a favorite stop in the 1970s and today

cooperative: sunny, with temperatures in the mid-eighties and low humidity, a day cooler and dryer than summer conditions usually were. Just plain gorgeous. Gihvan's Ferry State Park had dirt roads back then, and it still did. Like almost everything else in this area, it looked just the same. A song from James Taylor's *New Moon Shine* album called "One More Go 'Round" was playing in the headphones.

Back on the road, 61 led me toward 78. Somewhere near Wheatstone Crossroads, my low-fuel light came on, and where US 78 crosses US 301, I stopped to fill up and get a sandwich and a soda, quenching thirst of both man and machine.

I had been stopping to take photographs along the way, but by now I had used up the camera's digital storage capacity, so stops were fewer and chosen more judiciously. By 278, I was down to the last

in memory. They say "you can't go home again," but every once in a while, if you catch it just right, you can find yourself taking a truly unforgettable ride on The Road Back.

# NORTH GEORGIA COLORS

>>> This article was my first feature story for *Rider* magazine. It was first published in the magazine's April 2007 issue.

One of the best things about riding in northern Georgia is the relatively mild weather conditions the area experiences for three seasons of the year. This, coupled with the stunning fall colors that occur most years, can make for some of the best riding in the country. Since 2010 I have lived in the Seattle, Washington, area, and I have already discovered that the Pacific Northwest has many amazing roads to ride. Still, come fall time, I find myself yearning to ride these northern Georgia roads again, amid the blaze of red, orange, yellow, and gold foliage.

Left: Two motorcyclists on Georgia State Route 60
Above: A rider on State Route 75 in northern Georgia

SR 60 forms one of the legs of what is called the Georgia Triangle, found in northern Georgia. Riding the Triangle is a great way to see the state's fall foliage.

## Autumn Rides

The sunlight slid in on its autumn angle, backlighting a never-ending parade of yellow-, orange-, and red-leafed maples, oaks, poplars, and elms on the side of the mountain as I rode one of a hundred twisting roads in northern Georgia. Around every turn was another brilliant scene of electrified color—even the double yellow lines and orange diamond-shape road signs at the curves dovetailed with nature's massive color scheme. I found myself having to pull my eyes from the scenery and back to the road ahead, as these mountain roads were not to be taken for granted.

To motorcyclists of the Southeast, the roads of northern Georgia, southeastern Tennessee, and southwestern North Carolina are well known and frequently ridden. Much of the three-state area is contained within the Chattahoochee and Cherokee National Forests, protected and pristine, and any weekend day in spring, summer, and fall—with an occasional temperate winter's day thrown in—will find riders taking in the curves and scenery

It was the last weekend in October, and this was a particularly good year for the fall colors. The sun

A scenic sweep of road, State Route 52 runs east from Dahlonega, Georgia, a town that can serve as a base of operations for autumn rides in the area.

was coming in at an angled ecliptic, not from overhead, adding drama to the scenic views. The golden light illuminated a fully turned-out red and yellow forest through its leaves, intensifying these colors of the spectrum. Long shadows spilled across the road like a river overrunning its banks, and the sun was never in my eyes, but always behind and over my left shoulder.

In Georgia's autumn, temperatures can vary by 20 degrees or more from one day to another, with a constant tug-of-war between northern cold fronts and Gulf of Mexico–produced warming trends, until winter takes hold. As a result, daytime temperatures often reach the mid-seventies well into November. At 72 degrees, the day of my ride was just such a day, making for a perfect combination of comfortable riding conditions, great roads, and jaw-dropping scenery.

In this area, with the fall colors in full swing, the problem is not finding excellent and challenging roads with scenic views to ride but simply having the time to explore them all. As a native of Atlanta, I lived an hour's ride from North Georgia, so I set myself a task of taking several different routes over a three-day period to catalog and photograph some of the better-known riding roads in the area.

## Day One: The Triangle

Day one began with riding west on State Route 52 from SR 365, after traveling north from Atlanta for 52 miles. SR 52 west out of Lula is a fine riding road in its own right; the curves go from predominantly gentle to moderately challenging, warming you up as you continue west toward Dahlonega. The town of Dahlonega works well as a base of operations, allowing you to launch into any number of excellent day rides to the north, east, or west and still get back home by dinnertime. The town itself features several tourist attractions, such as Dahlonega Gold Museum, which tells the history of gold mining in Georgia. There are also several good restaurants and ice cream parlors. Within the town's borders are several of the better-known chain hotels (make reservations at this time of year!). Staying at one of these hotels puts restaurants and entertainment within walking distance so you don't have to get back on the bike.

Going north out of Dahlonega, US Route 19 leads to SR 60 toward the town of Suches. Any adjectives to describe riding this road at this time of year fail to adequately capture the experience. This road seems made for motorcycling, with its continual series of S-turns and diminishing-radius curves for the road's entire length; the incredible scenery on the 7 miles up to Suches, however, makes it difficult to fully concentrate on a road that requires 100 percent concentration. The intersection of SR 60 and US Route 19 marks the beginning of the three roads (SR 60, SR 180, and US 19) that make up the well-traveled riding circuit known as the Georgia Triangle. This 37-mile loop takes you through some of the best riding roads in the area and features the famous motorcycle-only campground and lodge known as Two Wheels Only (TWO), located in Suches, where SR 60 meets 180. It's a great location to launch into any of the many exhilarating roads throughout the Appalachian Mountain chain. [Update: After almost thirty years

Lake Winfield Scott, located in the campground of the same name, is an easy, half-hour motorcycle ride north from Dahlonega on SR 19, in the Georgia Triangle area.

of doing business, Two Wheels Only closed in March 2011 due to disputes with the land's new owners. While it is a true loss to the motorcycling community, some reports note that TWO may reopen or relocate to a nearby site. Check www.twowheelsonly .com for updates.]

Two Wheels Only Campground and Motorcycle Resort

In Suches, a right turn at SR 180, also known as Wolf Pen Gap Road, begins the Triangle's second leg, which is surely the most twisted piece of asphalt in North Georgia. With its reputation for having the sharpest turns and steepest grades of any road in the state, this 11-mile stretch is one of the coolest roads you will ever ride. It is a simply astonishing road when completely illuminated by the colors of autumn. SR 180 ends back at Highway 19, which will take you south to complete the 37-mile triangular loop or north toward the state's border.

Because of the abbreviated length of the days and the stops for photographs, the sun was low in the sky when I started the hour-and-a-half ride home. The weather for Sunday promised to be in the mid-sixties and clear, and I would be there again to enjoy them.

The rushing mountain stream and open landscape make this a good spot to take a riding break on State Route 60.

## Day Two: 175-Mile Loop

In the morning, I arrived back in Dahlonega, this time to head farther west on State Route 52 up toward Fort Mountain State Park, on a favorite ride of mine. The basic route will be west on SR 52 to Chatsworth to pick up US Route 411, which leads north across the Tennessee border to US 64/74 going east. This scenic highway passes through the Lake Ocoee and the Ocoee River areas on the southern end of Cherokee National Forest. There a turn onto North Carolina 68 South will lead back into Georgia to SR 60 and Suches, returning to Dahlonega on Highway 19. It is an ambitious 175-mile loop that will take four to five hours (depending on stops for fuel, food, and photographs).

I began the ride on SR 52 from Dahlonega to Ellijay in a relaxed (but still alert!) frame of mind, allowed by the sedate, gently curving road. This road borders the southern end of Chattahoochee National Forest, passing Amicalola State Park on the way, and the autumn show was in full swing for the entire 39-mile ride up to Ellijay.

Once through the town square of Ellijay, SR 52 begins the ascent up to Fort Mountain Park. While it is probably one of the lesser-ridden roads in North Georgia, SR 52 after Ellijay is easily one of the most enjoyable, full of challenging twisties and scenic stopping points. With the stunning color in the fall, it is as fine a road as any the state has to offer.

A few miles past Ellijay, I made a right turn on the road into Chattahoochee National Forest. Here, as the road ascended, the sun faced the mountain and moved slowly through an angled arc, shining through autumn colors and bathing the entire 25-mile length of highway in a bright golden glow. Once again, I find adjectives cannot fully capture the magical feeling of the surroundings, and while photographs can give you some idea, this is something that you have to see with your own eyes to fully appreciate. You find yourself saying the

Lake Trahlyta lies at the heart of Vogel State Park, which is the second oldest state park in Georgia. Vogel is located in Chattahoochee National Forest.

Riders travel scenic Hwy 64 in Tennessee.

word *wow* around every curve. As a photographer, I had to resist the impulse to stop every mile for photographs.

Once past Fort Mountain Park, the road descends 7 miles off the mountain and into the little town of Chatsworth, a good stop to fill up, get food, or just take a break, because once you're out of the area, options for stops become scarcer. From here I headed due north on US 411, a basic four-lane highway that allowed for some decompression time after the "rock and roll" of SR 52. The sedately undulating road let me kick back for 25 miles before the next few miles of twisting asphalt. On this road, I crossed the Tennessee state line and eventually reached the entrance of Tennessee's scenic Highway 64/74, which I rode toward the Ocoee River Basin.

Here, the tan color of the highway, also called Old Copper Road, contributes to the autumn scheme. Contrast is provided by the dark blue of Lake Ocoee and the river of the same name, which is famous for white-water rafting and kayaking. This highway offers leisurely viewing of the surroundings, with curves that are tranquil but winding enough

Named for the mined copper that was once transported along this route, Old Copper Road (Hwy 64) in Tennessee sweeps around Lake Ocoee.

Two kayakers ply the quiet waters of Lake Ocoee, near Tennessee's scenic Highway 64 .

to keep your interest. Be aware of pedestrians and vehicles loading and unloading kayaks around any turn, even in the autumn months, as well as the occasional slow-moving RV.

At about the 27th mile, I turned onto Highway 68 to go south through Grassy Creek and back over the Georgia state line at McCaysville. From there I picked SR 60 going south toward Suches; this leg is another of the most often ridden roads in North Georgia. It is a wonderful road with a continuous series of fairly extreme curve sets for all of its 37 miles back to Suches, with very few straight-line sections allowing you to catch your breath. From Suches, I take US 19 back to Dahlonega.

This loop constitutes a long ride, and some riders may be ready to call it a day before completing all 175 miles. Most towns along this route are of reasonable size with chain hotels available, so provided you call ahead (bring a hotel guide and a cell phone!), you can usually find lodging along the way, should you wish to extend it into a two-day ride.

October 29 saw the end of daylight savings time for the year, so peak sunlight occurred fairly early in the day, at about 2:30 p.m. The sun set at about 5:30 p.m., and in the mountains, the sun dropped behind the summits on the way to nightfall considerably sooner. With each passing hour after peak light, the sky turned progressively warmer toward the oranges and reds of all sunsets, deepening the colors everywhere around me. As I rode SR 60 south out of Suches, the yellow became gold, then muted orange, then red, and then violet. The day's end changed the fascinating scene with each passing minute before suddenly losing the light behind the mountain, finishing the visual concert like a symphonic finale.

While the last notes of the encore are certainly worth staying for, it is a good idea to remember that there is absolutely no artificial light up here. While that is, of course, the point, nightfall will bring a dangerous combination of dark, twisting mountain roads with few guardrails and steep drop-offs, and wildlife that lives everywhere in a national forest environment. As I timed it properly (more by luck than by planning), and with a full moon on the rise, the ride out of the mountains toward home proved as magnificent as the rest of the day.

Right: The trees on Georgia 60 seem ablaze as a rider winds through them. Overleaf: My BMW sport-touring motorcycle is parked on a particularly scenic roadside stop on SR 75 north of Helen, Georgia.

## Day Three: Around Helen

**M**y third riding day took me a few miles farther to the east, closer to the Bavarian town of Helen, Georgia. Many who live in the southeastern United States have heard of Helen, with its alpine-style chalets, German restaurants, and general Bavarian theme. A full complement of hotels, including mountain houses and cabin rentals, are available in this area. Many of the restaurants cater to motorcyclists, and any suitable weekend afternoon will find rows of motorcycles parked in front of establishments and watering holes all along State Route 75, the main drag through town. The area offers excellent riding roads leading into and out of the area, as well as several really fine circuit routes around Helen.

One such route, and my ride for the day, begins on the west side of town going north on Georgia 356, which passes the entrance of Unicoi State Park, before leading to GA 197, both truly excellent roads. The route heading north, with its moderately twisting roads and gorgeous scenery, was true to form that day, with lakes reflecting autumn colors and temperatures in the comfortable 70s—a rider's dream. Once again, I rode through Chattahoochee National Forest, guaranteeing a minimum of either residential or commercial development, save for a few cabin-rental businesses and minimally developed state parks designed to highlight the natural surroundings. Traffic was light, with more motorcycles than cars because of the roads' popularity with the two-wheeled set.

From there, I rode west on Highway 76 for 15 miles to pick up GA 75 again, heading south this time toward Helen. Both roads are highly recommended—Highway 76 for its more open, sedate curves, and GA 75 for its extreme ones. GA 75 also runs through the Anna Ruby Falls Scenic Area. It is an excellent loop ride any time of year, made far more enjoyable by the colors of the season.

Beautiful Unicoi Lake on SR 356, near Unicoi State Park

To extend the ride, when returning south on SR 75, make a right on GA Alternate 75 a mile before Helen. Continue south to GA 348, also called the Richard B. Russell Scenic Highway, which is another road not to be missed. This 14-mile scenic serpentine road runs near the top of the Appalachian chain here. It connects back to SR 180 and the Georgia Triangle area north of Dahlonega, bordering Unicoi State Park and crossing the Appalachian Hiking Trail on its way up to Maine in the process.

## More Days, More Roads

The briefest of glances at a Georgia map will reveal that there are many roads and areas that I have not been able to describe here. Three days of riding and 3,000 words allow neither the time nor the scope to cover many of the best roads in the area, let alone those in southern Tennessee and North Carolina. These are left for you to discover, and you'll find plenty of great ones. Loosely bordered by I-75 running northwest out of Atlanta, and I-985 going northeast, all of the roads north of Lake Lanier promise an excellent return on the investment, and most times of the year, they will provide some of the best riding you are likely to experience anywhere in the continental United States. But the autumn season offers all that with one of the best locales in the country for witnessing the yearly miracle of the fall colors. Make plans to see it on two wheels—it's something you'll never forget.

Inset: I stopped here for a more in-depth photo study of the trees off SR 75.
Right: Georgia 180 has the reputation for having the sharpest turns and steepest grades of any road in the state.

# NEW ROADS, NEW RIDES

>>> In October 2010, I relocated from Atlanta, Georgia, to the Seattle, Washington, area. On the week's drive across the country, I took the opportunity (with the help of my brother Joe, who drove the car pulling the trailer) to ride my bike on several of the travel days. I enjoyed some great rides, including one on the Mother Road, Route 66, and another through Lake Mead National Recreation Area.

After settling in Seattle, I wrote about my East Coast to West Coast experiences. *Baggers* magazine published an article about the cross-country move a year later in its October 2011 issue. This is that story, with a few more details not included in the piece when it was originally published.

Left: Riding through the Ozarks
Above: Beavertail cacti in bloom at Lake Mead National Recreation Area

# Changing and Moving On

**L**ife is about change. Accustomed to the routines in life, we may not often think about how quickly circumstances can, and sometimes do, change. As a resident of Atlanta, Georgia, for twenty-seven years, I had a familiar love-hate relationship with the city, knowing its good features and its bad, and making the city's Appalachian Mountain surroundings my riding turf since I had begun riding motorcycles as recreation, then as a way of life. Fairly recent layoffs for both my wife and me necessitated the sale of our home and led to the decision to let employment opportunities determine whether we would stay in Atlanta or live elsewhere.

"Elsewhere" ended up being some 2,700 miles away, when my wife, Lora, was offered a job in Seattle, Washington. You do what you must, and while she moved to Seattle in the early summer of 2010 to start work, I remained in Atlanta to organize the move of household goods and belongings. I promised myself that when it came time to make the trip, I would take the opportunity to ride through some of the areas of the country I had not had the chance to do so before. Thanks to my brother Joe (a resident of Punta Gorda, Florida), who volunteered to come along on the cross-country trip and drive the car pulling the bike-hauling trailer, I would be able to ride the bike on several days of the travel week.

Brother Joe with car and trailer at a roadside stop on Route 66

## The Journey Begins

**W**e began the cross-country trip on Sunday, October 17. It would be a long driving day to reach Rogers, Arkansas, where a good friend, Jodi Lightner, sales manager for the Aloft hotel, had offered to put us up in a room if we could get there by Sunday night. This made it an almost twelve-hour travel day, but we got to Rogers around 10 p.m. and were treated to a really great room at the Aloft, a very cool European-style hotel. Thanks to Jodi!

The town of Rogers is a nice surprise. Located off Interstate 540, it's an island of new construction with a surprisingly cosmopolitan feel. Rogers also features yearly motorcycling events that take advantage of the Ozark Mountains just east of town.

My motorcycle rests beside Fort Lake Smith, sheltered in the valley of the Boston Mountain Range of the Ozarks.

Monday dawned and brought a day of near-perfect conditions, with temperatures in the 70s and very low humidity—a beautiful autumn day in the mountains. I began my first riding day by going east on Arkansas 12 through the Beaver Lake area, passing through Prairie Creek and winding my way through Hobbs State Park before turning on AR 45, which headed south and then west into the foothill town of Fayetteville. With Joe ("lead singer, and driver of the Winnebago") trailering behind, I took US Route 71 South out of Fayetteville. US 71 is a fine country highway that runs along the western border of the Ozark National Forest, a great alternative to I-540 (the north-south interstate extension that runs just west of and parallel with 71) and the preferred choice for two-wheeled travel. Partway through the day, we stopped at the scenic Fort Lake Smith, a quiet lake in a valley of the Boston Mountain

Range of the Ozark Mountains that comes into view as you round a curve on the elevated highway. It is an inviting, clear blue pool that beckons a passerby to detour for a break, and we obliged.

The necessity of keeping to a schedule prevented my riding more of the recommended Ozark routes, but from what I saw on that afternoon's ride, the area is well worth a more thorough exploration. Next time, I guess. Arriving back at I-40, we put the bike on the trailer, traveled the interstate for the rest of the day, and stopped at Oklahoma City for the night.

The next day was a travel day, designed to get us farther west and allow more riding time on Wednesday. From Oklahoma City, a full day's drive past Albuquerque brought us to the small town of Grants, New Mexico. Studying the map after dinner, Joe found NM 53, a scenic loop road out of Grants

The petroglyphs at El Morro date back to at least the fourteenth century AD, when the Anasazi, ancestors of the Pueblo Indians, lived here.

that goes south and then west and features the state park El Morro National Monument.

On Wednesday morning, I got the bike off the trailer for the week's second ride. Like most highways in the southwestern states, NM 53 meanders through the desert foothills and a few small towns and is lightly traveled. El Morro National Monument is famous for Native American petroglyphs and more recent name and date carvings by various travelers and explorers who passed through the area. The more "modern" of these carvings date from 1605 into the mid-1800s, and the Native American petroglyphs certainly predate those. While I was taking in the sights, what looked to be an El Morro tarantula walked by, and I convinced him to pose for a picture.

Near the Arizona border, we got rain, which soon became sleet. At first I thought it was gravel on the road—until ice crystals started pelting me. Joe told

The hidden pool at the base of the 200-foot-high sandstone bluff made El Morro a popular oasis for travelers for many, many centuries.

An El Morro tarantula takes a moment to pose for a picture.

me later that he realized what the "white stuff" was when he saw a truck going in the other direction covered in ice. At that point, he looked back to catch me frantically flashing my bright lights and turn signals. Although he couldn't hear me, I was also yelling, "Joe, pull the car over, man! Pull the car over!" I usually try to deal with the weather as a part of the riding experience, but I draw the line at ice on the road. I was very glad that I had the option of putting the bike back on the trailer.

New Mexico 53 becomes Arizona 61 over the Arizona border and leads to US Route 191 North and back to I-40. After a short detour through the Petrified National Forest, we headed on to Flagstaff and got a room at the Courtyard by Marriott.